GOD

AND THE

NATIONS

GOD
AND THE
NATIONS

HENRY M. MORRIS

Master
Books

First printing: January 2002

ISBN: 0-89051-390-9
Library of Congress Number: 2002116466

Printed in the United States of America

Please visit our website for other great titles:
www.masterbooks.net

For information regarding author interviews, please contact the publicity department at (870) 438-5288.

ACKNOWLEDGMENTS

The writer appreciates the help of three of his children, all of whom are dedicated servants of the Lord and excellent Bible students: Dr. Kathy Bruce, a long-time missionary with Wycliffe Bible Translators; Dr. Henry Morris III, pastor and Bible teacher of over 35 years experience; and Dr. John Morris, ICR president since 1996 and author of several books of his own. All of these reviewed the manuscript and made good suggestions.

In addition, another daughter, Mary Smith, typed and edited the manuscript, as she has a number of other books of her father's, as well as several books by other ICR scientists.

Special thanks are due to Dr. Robert Sumner, the distinguished editor of *The Biblical Evangelist* and also a prolific writer and preacher. Dr. Sumner not only reviewed the manuscript but wrote a very kind foreword for the book.

TABLE OF CONTENTS

FOREWORD

There is a hoary story about two men taking a shortcut through a cemetery when one stopped and said to his friend, "Look, they've buried two men in this grave!" To the amusement of both, the tombstone read, "Here lies a lawyer and an honest man."

While this characterization, like most ethnic and professional jokes, is utterly untrue for many — some of our good friends are attorneys and as honest and truthful as the day is long — it might seriously be claimed that two men wrote this book. One author is a scientist and one is a theologian. Henry Morris is a respected scientist and has done more to bring the field of his profession back to the biblical position of a six solar-day creation than any other five men, leading the battle in repudiating humanistic evolution. At the same time he is a Bible student of amazing proportions, and whenever he picks up the Word of God to teach, his hearers are blessed, warmed, and amazed at his insight and knowledge as he unfolds what it teaches. In this work, Dr. Morris shows his deep knowledge of Bible history, biblical genealogy, and biblical etymology.

Yes, two men wrote this work: a thorough-going scientist of international repute, and a dedicated, humble Christian with a deep, clear understanding of The Book. Here is a professional scientist with an evangelist's burning passion for the souls of men, women, and youth. His chapter, "The Missionary Mandate," will leave no doubt whatsoever in the reader's mind.

Dr. Morris is one of my heroes. As a young preacher fresh out of seminary and in my first pastorate, during a day when the world was figuratively bathed in Darwinism from a cultural, sociological, and educational world view, I managed to get his little book, *That Ye Might Believe!* It thrilled my soul as had no book up to that point and I have referred to what I learned therein repeatedly through more than half a century. This, his latest work, deals with nations from the beginning of time in creation to time's closing as we know it. Christians will learn and profit from it while the unsaved *need* to read about their eternal destiny outside of Christ, then hopefully repent and believe (Acts 20:21).

Dr. Morris is unequivocally and unashamedly a believer in the inerrancy and authority of Scripture and he takes statements literally unless the context suggests otherwise. He is such an excellent Bible scholar and so saturates his thoughts with the Word of God, even if you disagree with something it will cause you to go back and re-examine your own position.

If someone asked you what God's purpose was in the nations of the world, what would you say? Most active Christians would be able to speak of His plan for Israel, but what about the other 200-plus nations in the world today? The purpose of this volume, Dr. Morris tells us, is to explain what God has said about the rise and fall of *all* nations, and His reasons behind those actions. Since most of those listed in God's "Table of Nations" (Gen. 10) no longer even exist, the author explains how God determined which ones would succeed and which would disappear from history. He deals with the spiritually "hot and cold" nation of Israel as well as the "times of the Gentiles," showing God's purposes in both. We thought his chapter on how nations began of special interest and value. Nimrod and Babylon come in for close scrutiny throughout the volume.

Do you have *questions*? Dr. Morris has *answers*. Some of the questions about nations with which he deals in this concise yet wide-ranging book include: What are the two principle mandates God gave all nations? To what regions did the sons of Noah migrate and develop nations? Who launched the other early nations? Why did God choose Israel as His elect nation? Why did He even need an elect nation? How does Paul's reference to the "times before appointed" refer to the early (and later) nations of the earth? What about America? Will it reach the "bounds" ordained by God and come to an end, too? What is the "dominion mandate" God has given *all* nations? Why does God put down one nation and establish another? What about the law of God? Does it apply to Christians today? Can any nation in the world in our day be described as truly seeking the God of the Bible and His Christ? Does God create evil among nations? If so, what kind? Is there a "gospel in the stars"? Should the prophecies about Christ's coming and God's wrath being poured out on the nations be taken literally or figuratively? How did God manifest His triunity in the universe? What form of government does God call for on the part of today's nations? Since God says all men are "without excuse," what universal witnesses are available to all the world's inhabitants? These and other questions are answered in this important, timely, and fascinating volume.

Islam is very much on the minds of the world's people today and Dr. Morris faces the issues it raises head on. He deals especially with the matter promoted by some religious leaders that "Allah" is just another name for the one true God, showing conclusively that it is not. While Islam holds to creation and some other biblical insights, for the most part it rejects its teachings, especially as to the person and work of our Lord Jesus Christ. Allah is no more the true God than is Baal or Ashtoreth, and the author notes that instead of being a synonym for Jehovah, the name "is really just another name for Satan."

That this is a very readable book should come as no surprise. Everything Henry Morris writes is highly readable and extremely profitable. We know of no other book like *God and the Nations* on this theme; it fills a real void in the Bible student's library. Actually, this might also be a good book to place in the hands of your senators and congressional leaders, along with those on the state and local levels. In fact, we recommend it.

In obtaining this work you made a wise purchase. It will help you in the days and years to come as you return repeatedly to reference its teaching.

Dr. Robert Sumner

INTRODUCTION

Behold, the nations are as a drop of a bucket, and are counted as the small dust of the balance (Isa. 40:15).

There have been many great nations in the history of the world. One thinks of Babylon and Assyria, of Greece and Rome, of Egypt. Then there was Napoleon's France and the great British Empire on which the sun never set. And now the United States of America, which Americans think is the greatest nation of all time. But what about China, with the largest population any nation ever had, and the vast Soviet Union, sprawled all over Europe and Asia? And the Muslim "Street," stretching almost from the Atlantic to the Pacific?

But God counts them as drops in a bucket and dust on a scale. *"All nations before him are as nothing, and they are counted to him less than nothing, and vanity"* (Isa. 40:17). God raises them up and puts them down, according to His own sovereign will, and *"who hath been his counsellor?"* (Rom. 11:34).

Yet God is not capricious. When nations rise and fall, there must be reasons. The question is, have these reasons been revealed in His written Word? It seems a question worth exploring in the deep and inexhaustible mine field of the Holy Scriptures. That is the purpose of this small exploratory volume.

There have apparently been few, if any, books on this subject, at least any currently available. Many volumes have been written about individual nations, of course, as well as regional and world histories, but even these are rarely written from the biblical perspective.

This is understandable. Readers naturally tend to be more interested in their own personal needs, so books tend to become more readily available which attempt to relate to *those* needs. For that matter, God himself is very much concerned with the individual person. Christ died, not just *"for the sins of the whole world"* (1 John 2:2), but also, as Paul said, He *"loved me, and gave himself for me"* (Gal. 2:20). We individual Christians are commanded to *"preach the gospel to every creature"* (Mark 16:15) and also to personally *"grow in grace, and in the knowledge of our Lord and Saviour Jesus Christ"* (2 Pet. 3:18). In fact, the New Testament especially is full of instructions concerning our personal beliefs and behavior.

Yet we should not overlook the fact that God is also vitally concerned with nations as such, as well as individuals. In fact, all the nations rejected Him, and therefore, He had to prepare a special nation, Israel, to preserve and convey His Word to the world. Nevertheless, there is coming a day when He *"will shake all nations, and the desire of all nations shall come"* (Hag. 2:7). Finally, when Christ does come again, every nation will turn back to the true God and *"all kings shall fall down before him: all nations shall serve him"* (Ps. 72:11).

The history of God's dealings with the nations — past, present, and future — is indeed a fascinating story, well worthy of study and understanding. The emphasis in the Bible, of course, especially the Old Testament, is on Israel as the chosen nation, but there is also a large amount of material about the Gentile nations. God certainly has never forgotten them and still has an eternal purpose for them. In fact, there are far too many passages dealing with the nations than can be expounded in this small book. Each chapter could well be expanded into a book itself and, for that matter, there have indeed been many books written about some of the topics that are here discussed briefly in individual chapters (e.g., the missionary mandate). But since the purpose here is to cover the whole history of all nations, and to do it strictly from a biblical viewpoint, a summary approach seems best at this time, emphasizing the key passages in particular.

To give an indication of the magnitude of biblical concern with the Gentile nations, the Hebrew word for "nations" (*goi*) occurs 556 times in the Old Testament and the Greek word (*ethnos*) 164 times.

The Hebrew word *goi* (*goiim* in the plural) is rendered "nations" 373 times, "Gentiles" 30 times and "heathen" 142 times. In the New Testament, *ethnos* is translated "nations" 64 times, "Gentiles" 93 times, "heathen" five times, and "peoples" two times.

The above number totals are as listed in *Young's Analytical Concordance of the Bible* and so should be accurate. In any case, they certainly indicate a significant interest in the nations. As would be surmised, the word "nations" is often synonymous with "Gentiles" or "heathen." Frequently, any of these three English words could be used interchangeably in a given passage, but not always. The best choice would depend on context (occasionally *goi* or *ethnos* is even applied to the nation of Israel, for example). In general, the King James translators have selected the most appropriate English word in any given passage, and we can understand the meaning accordingly.

It is nearly always best to take any given passage in its literal sense. Occasionally the biblical writer uses a word or phrase in a figurative or symbolic sense, but this will be evident in the context, and it is never right to insert some parabolic meaning into the text based on the reader's own imagination or bias. When the writers of the biblical text intended to use a figure of speech, this is always evident in the context, and the meaning of the figure is always given either in the immediate context or in the broader context of the Scriptures as a whole. This is the underlying assumption in interpreting the passages discussed and expounded in this book.

No attempt has been made to cite secular sources or even any other theological sources. The Bible seems to contain all that is relevant — or at least all that is really needed — for a comprehensive study of the origin, history, and destiny of the nations in their relation to God. One could say that this book as a whole is simply a survey of the biblical doctrine of the nations. We trust it will help lead Christians to a proper understanding of all nations and of their own nation in particular.

CHAPTER I

GOD'S PURPOSE FOR THE NATIONS

That God has an eternal purpose in mind for nations as such, and not only for individuals, seems evident from such Scriptures as Revelation 21:24:

> *And the nations of them which are saved shall walk in the light of it: and the kings of the earth do bring their glory and honour unto it.*

The context here is the situation in the New Earth, and the Holy City, New Jerusalem, in particular, in the eternal ages to come.

There will be *"nations"* in the New Earth, each with its "king," and they will live outside the Holy City, yet apparently have free access into it, with their *"glory and honour"* to contribute to the service of the King of all kings there in New Jerusalem. These nations will be "Gentile" nations, for the word "nations" (Greek *ethnos*) is actually translated "Gentiles" more often than "nations."

The nation Israel, on the other hand, as God's chosen nation, will occupy a separate position, presumably dwelling only in New Jerusalem. This seems implied by Revelation 21:12, which notes that *"the names of the twelve tribes of the children of Israel"* are inscribed on the 12 gates of New Jerusalem. Israel's "king," of course, will be their Messiah, the Lord Jesus Christ, who *"shall reign over the house of Jacob for ever"*

(Luke 1:33), and *"the throne of God and the Lamb shall be in it, and his servants shall serve him"* (Rev. 22:3).

The Church is also a "nation," in a sense, for Christian believers are actually called *"a royal priesthood, an holy nation"* in 1 Peter 2:9, and are considered as different in a sense from both Jews and Gentiles (see 1 Cor. 10:32, which refers to *"the Jews . . . the Gentiles"* and *"the church of God"*).

But all these relationships can be discussed in more detail later. At this point, we just want to get a glimpse of God's future purpose for the nations, because that will help us to understand His past and present dealings with them. When they were first established, and all through history, God was really preparing them for eternity. *"Known, unto God are all his works from the beginning of the world"* (Acts 15:18).

The Purpose of Creation

God's purpose for the nations obviously derives from His purpose in creating the world and its inhabitants. But how can we know this? *"For who hath known the mind of the Lord? or who hath been his counsellor?"* (Rom. 11:34).

The obvious response to this rhetorical question is that our limited human reason cannot possibly probe the infinite mind of God. We can only know *His* mind to the extent that He reveals His thoughts to us by some process of revelation. *"The secret things belong unto the LORD our God: but those things which are revealed belong unto us and to our children for ever, that we may do all the words of this law"* (Deut. 29:29).

That is, the *"secret things"* which God chooses to reveal to us are conveyed through the recorded *"words of this law,"* as written down in an earlier age by Moses and then in later times by David, Isaiah, John, Paul, and other God-called apostles and prophets. Once the final record was transcribed, the Book of Revelation, which carries us through God's plan for all the ages yet to come, His revelation of His selected secret things was complete, and it was closed with a serious warning not to delete anything from it or add anything to it (Rev. 22:18–19).

The fact is, however, that God has not chosen to reveal much about His purposes in creating the universe. It was simply His will to create.

The future testimony around His throne will be: *"Thou art worthy, O Lord, to receive glory and honour and power: for thou hast created all things, and for thy pleasure they are and were created"* (Rev. 4:11). The prophet Isaiah, quoting God especially of the future restoration of the dispersed nation of Israel, said, *"Even every one that is called by my name: for I have created him for my glory, I have formed him; yea, I have made him"* (Isa. 43:7).

And, speaking of Christian believers in the ages to come, the apostle Paul said that we have been saved through Christ, *"That in the ages to come he might shew the exceeding riches of his grace in his kindness toward us through Christ Jesus"* (Eph. 2:7).

Such hints may not spell out many details of God's great purpose in creation, but they do reveal that they come out of His nature of great love and grace. He has created a mighty and infinite cosmos, and myriads of fascinating and complex systems therein, and then created us *"in his image"* (Gen. 1:26), that we might share it all with Him forever. That is evidently enough for us to know right now. *"Eye hath not seen, nor ear heard, neither have entered into the heart of man, the things which God hath prepared for them that love him"* (1 Cor. 2:9).

These untold blessings are undoubtedly for individual believers, but somehow they must also be for the nations of those believers. *"Blessed is the nation whose God is the LORD"* (Ps. 33:12). *"And many nations shall be joined to the LORD in that day, and shall be my people"* (Zech. 2:11). *"Rejoice, ye Gentiles* [that is, 'nations'] *with his people"* (Rom. 15:10).

God's Record of Creation

The only means of really *knowing* anything about creation is by divine revelation. God was there, so He knows. No human scientist or historian was there, so they do not know. Evolutionary speculations of many varieties have abounded throughout human history, and some have formed the mythological basis of various religions, but they were all obtained either by human imagination or demonic deception.

The modern evolution myth — Darwinism — has served as the pseudo-scientific rationale for the religions of atheism, socialism, humanism, fascism, and even laissez-faire capitalism and imperialism, but it also is without any factual foundation, as thoroughly documented in numerous books by the present writer and many others (see, e.g., *The Long War Against God*, Master Books).

One possible way we can truly *know* anything about creation is for the Creator to tell us. Creation is not occurring now, so we cannot study the process in operation. In fact, the present processes of nature are all dominated by the two most certain laws ever discovered in science — the law of conservation in quantity of matter and energy, and disintegration of quality and availability of matter and energy. So far as we can learn, these two laws (also called the first and second laws of thermodynamics) have always been operating throughout history, so there is no possible way they can tell us about creation — except that it must have taken place at some time in the past by creative processes no longer in operation.

We are limited, therefore, to God's own record of creation for information about creation. That record, of course, is in the Book of Genesis, especially the very first chapter. The record has been rejected — even ridiculed — by skeptics of all ages, especially by modern intellectuals who claim it is unscientific, but it is the true record nonetheless. It was obviously intended to be understood as an actual historical account, probably written by the very hand of God himself (at least the first chapter, which describes events before the creation of the first man), and should be read literally, to mean exactly what it says. God is well able to say what He means!

That first chapter is climaxed by the account of the creation of Adam and Eve, the first man and first woman, *"in the image of God"* (Gen. 1:26–27). They were placed in charge of the creation that God had created, as God's stewards, and were also told to *"be fruitful and multiply and replenish* [that is, 'fill'] *the earth."* Although it would have been premature to talk about nations at that time, the future earth-filling population so envisioned would eventually need to be organized geographically in some way, and thus future nations are at least implied in this very first command of God.

This primeval "dominion mandate," as it has been called, will be discussed in more detail in the next chapter. It has never been withdrawn and its global importance is too little understood and appreciated today. However, today's nations are no less responsible for carrying out this mandate in the world we now live in than were Adam and Eve and their immediate descendants in the ancient world.

The creation itself was initially all *"very good,"* as so adjudged by God himself (Gen. 1:31). God had called into existence multitudes of animals of all kinds, to occupy the lands, the seas, and the atmosphere. He had covered the lands and ocean bottoms with grasses and shrubs and trees of all kinds, providing abundantly for all needs of the animate creation, as well as soils and nutrients of all kinds in which they could grow.

He had also filled the mighty cosmos with stars and groups of stars of all kinds, only a small fraction of which could actually be observed directly by early people, but all of which would be there for ultimate exploration and use in distant ages to come. In the meantime, the visible stars and constellations would serve, along with the sun and moon, to *"give light upon the earth"* and also to *"declare the glory of God"* and to *"be for signs and for seasons and for days, and years"* (Gen. 1:14–15; Ps. 19:1).

All of this was given to Adam and Eve and their descendants as a divine mandate of stewardship under God. Their central headquarters, so to speak, was to be the beautiful Garden of Eden, which God had planted especially as a home estate for this first husband and wife and their soon-coming family, but the whole earth was to be their dominion.

Once this was all accomplished, God *"rested from all his work which God created and made"* (Gen. 2:3). The work of "creating" (that is, calling into existence out of nothing but His own infinite power and knowledge) and "making" (that is, organizing the basic created materials into all manner of intricately complex systems and living organisms) was unimaginably great — in fact, beyond all measure and human understanding — but now it was done, so God *"rested."* He was not tired, of course, for *"the everlasting God, the Lord, the Creator of the ends of the earth, fainteth not, neither is weary"* (Isa. 40:28). But He simply stopped creating and making things, for all *"the works were finished from the foundation of the world"* (Heb. 4:3).

He had turned them all over to Adam and his future progeny to *"subdue"* — that is, to organize and govern as God's faithful steward, for the benefit of all His creatures, and for the honor and glory of God himself.

It was only in that sense that God rested. Actually, as the Lord Jesus would say many centuries later: *"My Father worketh hitherto, and I work"* (John 5:17). God's present work, however, is not that of creation or making (except occasionally in very special miracles) but of *conserving* what He had created — that is, keeping His cosmos from collapsing into chaos or nothingness. He is *"upholding all things by the word of his power"* (Heb. 1:3).

Furthermore, He soon had to undertake a new work — that of restoration. In spite of the perfect environment with all needs supplied, Adam and Eve soon yielded to the satanic temptation to *"be as gods, knowing good and evil"* (Gen. 3:5), and ate of the one fruit of the garden that had been placed off-limits by God. Thus, *"by one man, sin entered into the world, and death by sin"* (Rom. 5:12), so God, though Christ, began His age-long work of *"reconciling the world unto himself"* (2 Cor. 5:19).

That work, like the primeval work of creation, would eventually be completed also, and Christ would shout His great victory cry on the cross: *"It is finished!"* (John 19:30). And that work, like the first, would be followed by an age-long, worldwide mandate, this time a mandate, not of physical dominion, but of spiritual restoration. In a very real sense, God's present relationship with the nations of the world centers around these two great mandates. This fact will be the underlying theme permeating God's dealings with the nations.

From Creation to the Flood

Although Adam's sin had brought death into the world and God's general curse of decay on the whole creation (note Gen. 3:17–20; Rom. 8:20–22), men continued to live physically (although already dead spiritually) for many centuries. God had told Adam and Eve to multiply and they obeyed Him in that command even though they had rebelled against His command not to eat of the tree of knowledge of good and evil. Adam *"begat sons and daughters: And all the days that Adam lived were nine hundred and thirty years"* (Gen. 5:4–5).

The Bible does not give us the total number of his children, but there must have been many. Nine hundred and thirty years is a long time, and evidently most of these years were years of procreational ability. Enoch, for example, had a son at age 65 and Noah had three sons after age 500 (Gen. 5:21, 32).

The obvious implication from the genealogical data of Genesis chapter 5 is that world population expanded very rapidly, although no precise totals are given. Even very conservative birth and growth rates could easily yield a population of billions by the time of the Flood (1,656 years after creation, by the Ussher chronology).

However, there is no mention of any organized governmental or legal systems controlling these great masses of people, and eventually a state of practical anarchy developed. *"The earth also was corrupt before God, and the earth was filled with violence"* (Gen. 6:11), as well as filled with people. *"God saw that the wickedness of man was great in the earth, and that every imagination of the thoughts of his heart was only evil continually"* (Gen. 6:5).

It would surely have been better if society had been organized in governmental units of some kind, with means of preventing and punishing evil and violence. The only authority seems to have been patriarchal, but this was ineffective, and soon everyone seemed to be doing whatever he could get away with.

Possibly God was allowing this situation for a time in order to demonstrate to later generations the terrible depths of wickedness into which men and women could fall when unrestrained by fear of God or government. The situation was aggravated also when they yielded to the invasions and temptations of many fallen angelic *"sons of God"* — satanic angels attempting to corrupt all humanity by possessing the all-too-willing bodies of rebellious men and women, and then developing their progeny into giants — giants in both size and iniquity (see Gen. 6:1–4; also Jude 6–7).

Finally, God could tolerate it no longer, sending a terrible watery destruction to wash the earth clean, purging it of all its wicked human inhabitants, and banishing their spirits, along with all the rebellious angelic beings who had possessed their bodies, into an abyss deep in the heart of the earth to await God's final judgment.

This almost incredible depth of depravity had not come on instantaneously, of course. It began with what might have seemed a relatively harmless act of disobedience when Eve and Adam ate the fruit of a forbidden tree. They themselves repented and were forgiven, but the sin-nature with which their act had infected their very genetic systems would be transmitted to their children and all *their* children and indeed the whole human race. *"And so death passed upon all men, for that all have sinned"* (Rom. 5:12).

The first act of deadly violence manifested itself in Adam's own immediate family, when Cain slew his brother Abel. Whether or not Adam attempted to use his parental authority in judging Cain the record does not say, but there was no other authority to do so, except God. God would later ordain the system of capital punishment for murder (Gen. 9:6), but in Cain's situation, there had been no law-breaking as such, except in the human conscience, and no governmental authority to enforce it if there had been. Therefore, God himself intervened and invoked the punishment of banishment from Cain's parents and siblings. At the same time, He protected Cain from vengeance by any of these relatives, for they also were without law at the time and also possessed the inherited sin-nature (see Gen. 4:15).

Although the account in Genesis is brief, it does tell us that Cain had a number of younger brothers and sisters, possibly many of them even by that time (Gen. 5:4). Some of these may even have resented Abel as Cain had, but certainly others would have become very angry at Cain because of the murder. We do know also that Cain had taken one of his sisters as his wife and may well have had children of his own by this time.

Either at this time or soon afterwards, Cain had a son whom he named Enoch, meaning "dedication" or "commencement," probably signifying the abrupt change all this would mean in his life. Either from the families of his sympathetic siblings (if any) or from his own descendants, he built a "city," which he named after this particular son.

Undoubtedly, as the population grew, other communities would be built for social and commercial purposes, and they well may have developed around individual family groups. But there is no suggestion of any governmental structure and certainly there were no "nations" as such, in spite of the very large population that eventually *"filled the earth with violence."*

The only brief insight we get into a particular family in Cain's line — or that of any other son of Adam except Seth and the line of the

chosen *"seed"* — is that of arrogant and hostile Lamech and his polygamous marriage, a practice directly in flagrant disobedience to God's
primeval *"one flesh"* ordinance of marriage (see Gen. 4:19–24; 2:24).

The Godly Remnant

In all this morass of wickedness, however, there was one family
line which remained faithful to the Creator in spite of all the temptations and general ungodliness surrounding them. This, of course, was
the line from Seth to Noah. Adam and Eve recognized that God had
chosen Seth to replace Abel, who had himself been a *"prophet"* of God
(Gen. 4:25; Luke 11:50–51), and was a true man of faith (Heb. 11:4),
believing God's promises and obeying God's will.

Seth followed in Abel's footsteps and taught his own son Enos, in
whose time *"began men to call upon the name of the Lord"* (Gen. 4:26),
probably implying the practice of prayer. Enos actually lived all through
the time of Enoch, his great-great grandson, and probably took part in
the spiritual training of Enoch, as well as the others leading to Enoch
(Cainan, Mahaleel, and Jared).

Enoch in turn was such a godly man that he *"walked with God"*
and finally *"was translated that he should not see death"* (Gen. 5:24;
Heb. 11:5). He was also a strong witness against the increasing wickedness of all his contemporaries — not only among Cain's descendants
but also in those from Adam's other sons and daughters (including
even other descendants of Seth, no doubt, since by Noah's time (Noah
was born just 69 years after Enoch's translation) practically the whole
world was engulfed in evil and violence. Note the excerpt from one of
Enoch's messages as preserved in Jude 14, 15.

Enoch's own son, Methuselah, lived until the very year of the Flood
and no doubt was instrumental in teaching his own son, Lamech, and
grandson Noah. Lamech was a godly man who made an inspired prophecy concerning what God would do through his son Noah (Gen. 5:28–30).

And Noah, of course, *"found grace in the eyes of the Lord,"* and
"walked with God" (Gen. 6:8–9). It was in Noah's time that God finally
had to *"destroy man whom I have created from the face of the earth"*
(Gen. 6:7).

Noah, therefore, was chosen by God to preserve life through the
Flood — both human life and all air-breathing animal life — in a great

vessel as specified by God, with optimum dimensions that would keep the vessel safe and tolerably comfortable through the year-long world-wide inundation.

And so, as confirmed by Christ, *"the flood came, and took them all away"* (Matt. 24:39). Peter later added that *"the world that then was, being overflowed with water, perished"* (2 Pet. 3:6). The remnant preserved on the ark would give mankind a new start. This time there *would be* laws and nations and governments, and men would be responsible to obey them, with retribution otherwise.

CHAPTER II

THE DOMINION MANDATE

Although God's elect nation was Israel and in this age is the Church, the Gentile nations are still in view in His eternal plan for His creation. When Adam and Eve were first created, God gave them a very specific command, and this has never been withdrawn. It was obviously intended for all their descendants as well as for Adam and Eve themselves. That command was as follows:

> *And God said, Let us make man in our image, after our likeness: and let them have dominion over the fish of the sea, and over the fowl of the air, and over the cattle, and over all the earth, and over every creeping thing that creepeth upon the earth. So God created man in his own image, in the image of God created he him; male and female created he them. And God blessed them, and God said unto them, Be fruitful, and multiply, and replenish the earth, and subdue it: and have dominion over the fish of the sea, and over the fowl of the air, and over every living thing that moveth upon the earth* (Gen. 1:26–28).

This primeval commandment has been variously called the Edenic Mandate, the Adamic Mandate or — most appropriately — the Dominion Mandate. It clearly specifies that Man (Adam and his descendants) is to have full dominion (under God, of course) of the entire earth and all its creatures. No details are given as to *how* this dominion was to be exercised, but it certainly was intended as a stewardship, not a despotism.

Apparently, Adam was himself to be in charge at the beginning, and the only "nation" he would govern would be his own family as the population began to multiply.

Part of the mandate, in fact, was to *"be fruitful and multiply,"* and God had a wonderful provision for this to be accomplished through the amazing process of procreation. Obviously, a large population would be necessary if the rest of the mandate were to be carried out. God had said they were to exercise dominion *"over all the earth,"* and for this to be done, they would first have to *"fill the earth."* The Hebrew verb *male,* translated *"replenish"* in the standard authorized English version (commonly called the "King James Version"), actually means, simply "to fill," which was the original connotation also of the English verb "replenish." That is, there had been no previous inhabitants on the earth, for Adam was the *"first man"* and Eve was *"the mother of all living"* (1 Cor. 15:45; Gen. 3:20). The earth itself was only six days old, so the people needed to *"subdue"* it would all have to come from Adam and Eve.

It is noteworthy that, although no provision for a formal system of human governance was established at that time, the most basic of all human institutions — that of marriage and the home — *was* set up.

> *And the LORD God said, It is not good that the man should be alone; I will make him an help meet for him. . . . And the rib, which the LORD God had taken from man, made he a woman, and brought her unto the man. . . . Therefore shall a man leave his father, and his mother, and shall cleave unto his wife: and they shall be one flesh* (Gen. 2:18–24).

This primeval principle of the home — one man and one woman united for life — was reaffirmed thousands of years later by the Creator himself, the Lord Jesus Christ. In response to a question about marriage and divorce, He said:

> *Have you not read, that he which made them at the beginning made them male and female, And said, For this cause shall a man leave his father and mother, and shall cleave to his wife: and they twain shall be one flesh?* (Matt. 19:4–5).

Scope of the Mandate

The command to subdue the earth is very broad in terms of authorized vocations, apparently covering practically every honorable human occupation. The verb "subdue" does not necessarily connote an unruly creation needing to be restrained and subjugated, like a wild horse, for everything was created *"very good,"* but does imply "control" of its resources and processes in an orderly fashion, and this in turn would mean diligent study and work on man's part.

To control them, men must first learn to understand them, and this would entail study and research. All the disciplines which we now call *science* (physics, chemistry, biology, geology, etc.) would inevitably be developed as men studied and sought to understand how these processes worked.

Before they could really be subdued or controlled for use in the service of mankind, however, the disciplines we now identify as *technology* (engineering, medicine, agriculture, etc.) would need to be developed. For effective implementation of science and technology, many other vocations would eventually be organized. These would collectively be called *commerce* (construction, transportation, business, shipping, trade, etc.). The various service industries would thus also be included under this dominion mandate. The profession of education would also be needed in order to transmit these skills to future generations.

It would also be appropriate for the fine arts to be instituted with the high purpose of glorifying the Creator and the wonders and beauties of His creation. Thus would come into being the vocations of music, art, literature and others. All other honorable occupations could be subsumed under the dominion mandate in the original *"very good"* (Gen. 1:31) world that God had created, although at that time there theoretically would be no need for such occupations as the military, law enforcement, or other such governmental agencies.

In fact, as far as the record goes, in the Edenic world as intended by the Creator, there would have been no government necessary at all, except the patriarchal system, with the father as head of each family and with his wife as a *"help"* meet for him. Presumably as each son grew to manhood and took a wife, he would then *"cleave to"* her, leaving his father and mother and thus establishing his own family unit.

Society thus would eventually consist of many families, each with its own head, working together to honor God and serve mankind.

But such an idyllic society never actually existed, because Satan and the entrance of sin into the world complicated the world before the process of filling it could begin.

The most basic of all human occupations, of course, would be that of farming. In this original idyllic world, it was intended that man, as well as animals, would all be vegetarians, living off the food that could be obtained from the ground. God had said:

> *Behold, I have given unto you every herb bearing seed, which is upon the face of all the earth, and every tree, in the which is the fruit of a tree yielding seed; to you it shall be for meat. And to every beast of the earth, and to every fowl of the air, and to every thing that creepeth upon the earth, wherein there is life, I have given every green herb for meat, and it was so* (Gen. 1:29–30).

The very next verse tells us that *"God saw every thing that he had made,"* including this worldwide provision of renewable food resources for both men and animals, and that it was all *"very good"* (Gen. 1:31). Since there was an abundance for everyone, and all easily attainable, there was no need of any "struggle for existence." Adam merely had the luxurious Garden of Eden for his immediate home and all he had to do to earn his living, so to speak, was *"to dress it and to keep it"* (Gen. 2:15). With the entrance of sin and God's curse on the ground, however, (Gen. 3:17), his work became far more rigorous.

Later on, other occupations were developed, as families grew and different needs developed. The first sons of Adam and Eve were Cain and Abel. Cain continued in the occupation of his father, as *"a tiller of the ground,"* whereas Abel became the first husbandman, as *"a keeper of sheep"* (Gen. 4:2), not for food, of course, but for clothing and presumably for sacrifice.

Then, still later, Cain *"builded a city,"* implying that he and his own descendants developed still other crafts. One man, named Jabal, developed tentmaking, and his brother Jubal invented musical instruments. Tubal-cain learned how to forge and manufacture metallic instruments for various uses (see Gen. 4:17, 20–22).

No doubt many other trades were devised during the antediluvian period. Men were highly intelligent, lived hundreds of years, and probably developed a high civilization in the almost two millennia before God sent the great Flood to destroy it all. Noah was able to build a huge ark, and, soon after the Flood, Nimrod and his subjects constructed a great tower, as well as a number of cities.

They were not primitive ape-like savages, as the evolutionary anthropologists would like us to believe, but brilliant and powerful men. After all, in order to fulfill His dominion mandate, God had equipped them with the intrinsic abilities needed to subdue the earth and have dominion over it as He had intended. Even though they may have forgotten the mandate itself, they were in effect carrying it out as the population grew.

There were apparently no nations as such. All people continued to speak the same language as used by Adam and Eve and by God himself back in the Garden of Eden. Presumably some of the family heads (like Cain) built communities of houses for their children, and various shops and even manufacturing industries may well have started in these communities, but there were no rulers as such, except the patriarchal heads of the different clans, at least as far as recorded or implied in the Genesis record.

Anarchy in the World

Men, however, were not only highly intelligent and inventive, but also wicked. They had inherited a sin-nature from Father Adam and Mother Eve, and this increasingly manifested itself in the advancing generations. It had produced the first murder when Cain killed Abel and the first (recorded) polygamous marriage when Lamech married Adah and Zillah (Gen. 4:8, 19), and it was not too long before *"the wickedness of man was great in the earth"* (Gen. 6:5). Enoch, in the seventh generation from Adam, was called to preach against this ungodliness, with the gist of his message preserved in the Book of Jude.

> *Behold, the Lord cometh with ten thousands of his saints, To execute judgment upon all, and to convince all that are ungodly among them of all their ungodly deeds which they have ungodly*

*committed, and of all their hard speeches which ungodly sinners
have spoken against him* (Jude 14–15).

There seem to have been no governmental restraints to deal with
these *"ungodly deeds"* that men were committing against each other,
and soon *"the earth was filled with violence"* (Gen. 6:11), and a state of
anarchy prevailed everywhere.

The situation was fearfully aggravated when the ungodly men and
women filling the world became vulnerable even to demonic possession. Satan and his hosts of rebellious angels had been hoping to over-
throw God and His holy angels right from the beginning (and still cher-
ish that hope, incidentally). This rebellious anarchy on earth gave them
the greatest and most nearly successful opportunity to do so that they
have ever had.

*The sons of God came in unto the daughters of men, and they
bare children unto them* (Gen. 6:4).

This development seems so incredible that many Bible expositors
have tried to explain it away by devising naturalistic interpretations —
calling *"the sons of God"* either descendants of Seth or great antediluvian kings and assuming *"the daughters of men"* either to be descendants of Cain or of commoners. Neither so-called explanation is based
on biblical data, of course, either in the immediate context or anywhere else in the Bible.

If we let the Bible mean what it says, then these sons of God were
fallen angels. The specific phrase, *"sons of God"* is used in the Old Testament *only* to refer to angels (note Job 1:6; 2:1; 38:7; Dan. 3:25; Ps.
29:1; 89:6). In the New Testament, it is used either to refer to Adam, to
Christ (neither of whom had a human father), or to those who have
become spiritual sons of God by the new birth.

The New Testament does speak of these fallen angels and of this
very event. *"God spared not the angels that sinned, but cast them down
to hell, and delivered them into chains of darkness, to be reserved unto
judgment"* (2 Pet. 2:4). *"The angels which kept not their first estate, but
left their own habitation, he hath reserved in everlasting chains under
darkness unto the judgment of the great day"* (Jude 6).

But scholars object that it would be impossible for angels to have
children with human women and for the women to have children be-

gotten by these angels. Satan's purpose, however, was not sex, but corruption and control, desiring to prevent the promised *"seed of the woman"* from being born in the human family to destroy him and his angels, as God had promised (Gen. 3:15), and perhaps also to enlist the human race in his own ongoing rebellion against God. When the biblical account says that these sons of God (sons by creation, not regeneration) *"took them wives"* (Gen. 6:2), we can understand it as "took them women," since the words "wife" and "woman" are translations of exactly the same Hebrew word. There was no wedding involved in such unions, but merely possession and control. The fallen angels are the demons, and the phenomenon probably simply involved demon possession. The children born to these demon-possessed women were thereby also demon-possessed and demon-controlled. Their human fathers may well also, by virtue of their wickedness, have been under the control of demonic spirits. By some unexplained nutritional process, these demon-possessed infants were then developed by their wicked fathers and "god fathers" into physical giants and giants of wickedness.

When all this physical and moral monstrosity became globally rampant, Satan may have thought he was on the verge of winning his war with God. If so, he was wrong, but God's remedy was drastic. As the Lord Jesus Christ later would say, *"The flood came, and destroyed them all"* (Luke 17:27).

The world has never, before or since, seen a cataclysm such as this, when *"all flesh died that moved upon the earth. . . . All in whose nostrils was the breath of life, of all that was in the dry land, died"* (Gen. 7:21–22). *"The world that then was, being overflowed with water, perished"* (2 Pet. 3:6).

By the time of the Flood, almost two thousand years after Adam's sin, the population of the world was probably of the same order of magnitude as it is today. This can very easily be demonstrated by using present-day population statistics, remembering that men and women lived hundreds of years and had children through most of their lives. The Bible twice says *"the earth was filled with violence"* (Gen. 6:11, 13), and thus it would first have to be filled with people.

The tremendous sediments eroded, transported, and redeposited during the Flood can often harbor the fossilized remains of creatures drowned and buried in the waters of the Flood. Sadly, these have been widely reinterpreted to fit the preferred model of evolutionary geology representing the life forms of various alleged geological ages. Very few human fossils have been found in the sediments of the Flood, however, since the inhabitants of the ancient world probably would have been buried and preserved, if at all, in the deposits now at the bottom of the oceans. In fact, most of them would never have been buried at all, but rather floated as corpses on the water surfaces and finally rotted away after washing up on the ancient shore. Those human fossils that *have* been found generally date from some local catastrophe that buried them many years *after* the Flood itself.

With the exception of eight people (Noah, his three sons, and their wives), Satan had indeed corrupted all living people by the time God sent the Flood, but Noah had *"found grace in the eyes of the* Lord,*"* and God had not been defeated after all. He would simply start over again, with Noah instead of Adam, in a vastly different world than had been given to that first man back in Eden.

The Renewed Mandate

God had not failed in His purpose in creation, of course, for He cannot fail. However, man had failed. In one way, the dominion mandate had partially been carried out, for mankind had indeed been fruitful and multiplied and filled the earth, but it had been filled with wickedness and violence. A degree of knowledge and culture had been achieved and dominion *was* being exercised over the earth as a result, but not as a stewardship under God, for God was being ignored and opposed. It became so bad that God had to wash the earth clean and start over with the one man Satan had been unable to corrupt.

God's long-range purpose had not been altered, so He simply renewed the dominion mandate to Noah and *his* descendants, after first promising He would never send such a global flood again.

God blessed Noah and his sons, and said unto them, Be fruitful,
and multiply, and replenish [that is, "fill"] *the earth* (Gen. 9:1).

This was the same command as originally given Adam (Gen. 1:28), but instead of simply telling Noah to have dominion over the animals (God did tell him that they were *"delivered"* unto his hand — Gen. 9:2),

God had placed a new fear and dread of mankind on the animals, and even gave men the authority to use animals, as well as plants, for food. This implies that animals also could become carnivores if the depleted environments of the post-Flood world should warrant it. Presumably the Flood had largely depleted the primeval soils and atmosphere of nutrients needed by man and some of the animals, and the climates were more rigorous than before, so that more proteins and other nutrients were needed than available in a post-Flood herbivorous diet. However, man was not authorized to eat animal flesh with blood, which represented its life (Gen. 9:4).

Then one very significant component was added to the mandate. God would no longer allow man the freedom to descend into anarchy as had happened before.

> *Whoso sheddeth man's blood, by man shall his blood be shed* (Gen. 9:6).

This very simple addendum in effect authorized the establishment of human government, as needed to restrain and punish the types of wickedness and violence that had led to such chaos in the antediluvian world.

This new command did not specify the *type* of government, but only its main function. Although it only seems to proscribe one particular crime, that of murder, in effect it implies authority to control whatever other kinds of behavior might lead to murder — that is, such crimes as robbery, adultery, rape, battery, slander, blackmail, and others.

Such controls could be implemented by means of a monarchy, a democracy, an oligarchy, or a theocracy or perhaps others, depending on the people and circumstances involved. In any case, some kind of government would be necessary, and this would imply that many new types of vocations were now called for.

Not only government bureaucrats, but also policemen, judges, lawyers, legislators, and others necessary for a functioning government are implied. Some kind of military establishment is also warranted.

Thus, the dominion mandate not only authorizes but anticipates every form of human activity that is honorable and useful in the service of God and man. This mandate has never been withdrawn and so is incumbent still upon all men, regardless of their nation (in fact, the mandate dates back before individual nations had even been established) or religion or anything else.

One does not have to be a professional religionist, therefore to be in service to God. *"Whatsoever thy hand findeth to do, do it with thy might"* (Eccles. 9:10). *"Whatsoever ye do, do it heartily, as to the Lord"* (Col. 3:23). *"Whether therefore ye eat, or drink, or whatsoever ye do, do all to the glory of God"* (1 Cor. 10:31). One can be an engineer, or homemaker, or sales clerk, or accountant, or most anything and be as much a part of God's plan as if he or she were a missionary or pastor or in any of the so-called full-time religious vocations. It all depends on the gifts and calling of God. At the judgment seat of Christ, *"the fire shall try every man's work of what sort it is"* (1 Cor. 3:13), not how big it is or what vocation it is. The Lord Jesus cares more about our motives and our love, not so much about our particular profession or standing therein.

CHAPTER III

How the Nations Began

T he Bible makes it very clear that, originally, there was only one
nation, just as there is only one race — the human race. *"The
whole earth was of one language, and of one speech"* (Gen. 11:1).

That is certainly not how it is today. There are over 200 organized
nations in the world, with clearly delineated territories and over 6,600
distinct languages and dialects corresponding to different ethnic groups
within those nations.

How could such a drastic change occur, especially in the short
time span indicated for human history as recorded in the Bible? It
couldn't, of course, by any natural process of language "evolution,"
and the Scriptures reveal that the confusion of tongues took place instantaneously and supernaturally as a result of a great event at the first
Babylon.

Among the children of Ham was Cush, and one of *his* sons was
named Nimrod, a name which seems to have meant "Let us rebel"
(the Hebrew word for "rebel" was *marad*), and Nimrod *"began to be
a mighty one in the earth"* (Gen. 10:8). As the population multiplied,
he eventually acquired a position of preeminence among the descendants of Noah, and founded several cities in the region of
Mesopotamia known to archaeologists as Sumer (Shinar in the
Bible). The chief city was Babel (later called Babylon), but his rule
extended through the entire region known later as Sumeria and eventually Babylonia and Assyria. In fact, his very name is apparently
preserved, not only in the city long known as Nimirud, near Nineveh,

but probably even in the name Marduk (or Merodach), the chief God of the later Babylonians.

In any case, perhaps fomented by his father, Cush, and even by his grandfather Ham, he undertook to lead a tragic rebellion against God and His dominion mandate. Instead of "filling the earth," and organizing its resources and systems as a divinely given stewardship, he tried to keep the entire population centralized in and around Babel, in order to *"make us a name, lest we be scattered abroad upon the face of the whole earth"* (Gen. 11:4). This purpose was obviously in direct opposition to God's command to fill the earth.

As the nerve-center of Babel, he decided to build a great *"tower whose top may reach unto heaven"* (Gen. 11:4). However, the words *"may reach"* were not in the original, and have misled many expositors, both ancient and modern, to misunderstand the evil purpose of Nimrod and his followers. Nimrod was not so foolish as to think his tower could actually reach God's home in heaven, nor would his purpose be to build such a high tower that people could escape a future deluge (he knew God had promised Noah never to send such a flood again).

Almost certainly his purpose was to build a great "high place" which could be used as a shrine dedicated to worshipful communication with the angelic host of Satan, the army of demonic spirits (fallen angels) later called by the apostle Paul *"the rulers of the darkness of this world,"* the *"principalities and powers"* governing all the *"spiritual wickedness in high places"* (Eph. 6:12; Col. 2:15) — perhaps even to communicate with Satan himself in order to participate on the human level with Satan in Satan's own war against God.

Signs in the Stars

On the fourth day of creation week, God had made the stars and placed them in the sidereal heavens, extending far out into space. Only about 4,000 or so of these stars can be seen with the naked eye, but the modern giant telescopes have revealed innumerable galaxies of stars in every direction as far as the telescopes have been able to penetrate. Whether there is an end to them, no one knows. As God says, *"For as the heavens are higher than the earth, so are my ways higher than your ways, and my thoughts than your thoughts"* (Isa. 55:9). Although it would be impossible humanly to actually *count* the stars, the number has been estimated statistically to be on the order of 10^{25}, a number inconceivably large (ten trillion trillion).

Even more amazingly, the Lord *knows* each of the stars and has given each one a name. God *"bringeth out their host by number. He calleth them all by their names"* (Isa. 40:26). It seems certain that He somehow has a particular purpose for each one in the eternal ages to come, for He is not a capricious God. We do know that each star is individually different from all the rest, for each will plot at a different spot on the so-called Hertzsprung-Russell Diagram, which means it has its own unique combination of stellar magnitude and temperature.

Whatever may be their future purpose, those stars visible to the naked eye were said by God to have been uniquely placed in the heavens not only *"to give light upon the earth"* but also to *"be for signs, and for seasons, and for days, and years"* (Gen. 1:14–15).

To measure seasons, days, and years, they would need to orbit the earth daily (or to *appear* to orbit the earth as the latter rotates daily on its axis) and also to travel annually along a celestial line called the ecliptic (or to *appear* to do so as the earth travels annually around the sun).

But just how could they serve as "signs"? Signs of what? Whatever they were intended to signify, they would need to be specifically placed by God in the heavens in locations and combinations that would serve this purpose, and then their purpose and meaning somehow revealed to man.

The fact that God did, indeed, have some such purpose in mind is confirmed by certain passages in the ancient Book of Job (probably the oldest of all books of the Bible, with the exception of the first 11 chapters of Genesis). Note the following verses and their implications.

[God] *alone spreadeth out the heavens. . . . What maketh Arcturus, Orion, and Pleides, and the chambers of the south* (Job 9:8–9).

By his Spirit he hath garnished the heavens; his hand hath formed the crooked serpent (Job 26:13).

Canst thou bring forth Mazzaroth in his season? or canst thou guide Arcturus with his sons? (Job 38:32).

Now Orion, Pleides, the crooked serpent, the chambers of the south, Arcturus and his sons, are all particular groupings of stars, or constellations — identified as such by nations everywhere from remotest antiquity. The most significant reference, however, is that of bringing forth Mazzaroth in his season. The term Mazzaroth, used only in Job 38:32, almost certainly is a reference to the 12 signs of the zodiac, as they come into prominence, one by one, month after month, in the sky. These are associated now with the pseudo-science of astrology, which is unequivocally condemned in the Bible (e.g., Isa. 47:12–14).

Nevertheless, as implied in God's rhetorical question to Job, these "signs of the zodiac" had originally been established by God. It is eminently reasonable to infer that these zodiacal signs were originally among the "signs" involved in God's primeval purpose for the stars (Gen. 1:14). Therefore, they were intended to convey information of some kind to Adam and his descendants.

This is further indicated by the fact that these signs of the zodiac, as well as the many other constellations, bear no resemblance whatever to the figures associated with them. They could never have been invented by early man on the basis of any similarity to those figures. Rather, the pictures must have been specifically assigned to the respective star groupings simply as an aid to remembering the meanings intended to be conveyed by the signs. Those meanings are obviously not the meanings and uses assumed by astrologers, since astrology as such has been strongly condemned by the one who created the star groupings in the first place.

What, then, were the meanings originally intended by God for these signs? Also, who originally expounded them correctly, and when and how and by whom were they corrupted into astrology?

These questions bring us back to Nimrod and his tower for the probable answers. Remembering that Satan's ultimate goal is to take over God's universe and also that he is the father of all liars, we almost have to assume that Satan was behind Nimrod's rebellious plans. Satan had enlisted a third of the vast angelic host in his rebellion (see Rev. 12:4, 9) and had apparently been able also to recruit Nimrod and his lieutenants, hoping thereby to bring the entire human race under his control, so that God's primeval promise of a coming Savior (Gen. 3:15) could be thwarted.

A number of keen Bible students of the 19th century were convinced that the message of the stars reflected that primeval promise and other related divine revelations given to Adam and other patriarchs. These included E.W. Maunder, the eminent British astronomer, and such great theologians as Joseph Seiss and E.W. Bullinger. Long before them, however, the Jewish historian of the time of Christ, Josephus, had written that the stellar gospel had first been written down by Seth, the son of Adam.

Whatever the details of its origin were, it is noteworthy that many ancient myths, including those involving the star signs (the virgin, the lion, the ram, etc.) seem to reflect the protevangelic promise of Genesis 3:15 in various ways, especially the ultimate triumph of a virgin-born hero defeating the old serpent after first being seriously wounded by him.

If, indeed, the stars had been so invested with an indelible transcription of God's great purposes for His creation, it would have served the ancient generations as a sort of Bible. The actual books of our present Bible did not begin to be recorded until the time of Job and then Moses. Such a revelation in the heavens could not have been erased even by the waters of the coming global deluge — which also was later memorialized in one or more of the constellations.

Satan could not obliterate the star-figures, of course, but he could corrupt their message, and this was what he probably did through Nimrod. The great human rebel seems to have somehow been in communication with Satan, the brilliant angelic rebel, who had been able to corrupt God's message to Eve long before he approached Nimrod.

Thus Nimrod became a key leader on the human level in Satan's age-long heaven-centered conspiracy against the Creator. Whatever may have been the original sign-message recorded in the sequence of constellations in Mazzaroth, Satan and Nimrod corrupted into the vast pagan religious system built around astrology. Idolatry soon followed, with the idols representing the star figures, enabling men and women to worship the *"host of heaven"* — none other than Satan and his angels — those whom the Bible calls the principalities and powers in the heavens, Satan himself being *"the prince of the power of the air"* (Eph. 2:2).

As the apostle Paul made clear, those who worship idols are not just worshiping sticks and stones, but worshiping demons (1 Cor. 10:20), thereby opening themselves to actual spiritual communication with the evil spirits who lurk in and around the idols. Thus, spiritism is connected with idolatry and astrology and the worship of the Satanic *"host of heaven,"* so vigorously condemned and forbidden by the Word of God (e.g., 2 Kings 17:5–18, esp. v. 16).

It is highly probable that all these characteristics of pagan religion were instigated and instituted at the Tower of Babel by Nimrod, in consultation with Satan. They began with the reinterpretation of the heavenly signs which had been intended to preserve the divine revelatory promise of Eden, changing them into the great deception of astrology, a system allegedly able to guide human beings in their personal lives here on earth. All of this may seem diabolically reasonable in light of the fact that the angelic hosts of heaven probably have their basic dwellings among the stars in the stellar host of heaven. Angels are sometimes even called "stars" in the Bible, presumably because they live there. In this sense, the stars might well seem to control and guide human lives, and the so-called science of astrology can achieve a powerful hold on the minds and decisions of men.

When Nimrod built his Tower of Babel *"unto"* the heavens, we can infer that the shrine at its apex was thus dedicated to worshiping and communicating there with the satanic hosts in their warfare with God. That shrine was probably emblazoned with the signs of the zodiac on its walls and ceiling, as is known to have been the case with many of the ziggurat towers in Babylonia and elsewhere which were built later in emulation of the Tower of Babel. In that great tower, Satan taught Nimrod and Nimrod taught his human followers the pagan religious system of Satan's conspiracy.

We cannot *prove* the above scenario, but it does make sense in seeking to understand the long war of Satan against God in all of its aspects. No wonder Babylon is called *"the mother of harlots and abominations of the earth"* (Rev. 17:5), for that original Babylon is where all the false religions of the world (that is, spiritual harlotry) and idolatries of the world (the basic meaning of "abominations") began in the present world under Nimrod long ago. All such religions even today parrot Satan's lie that the true God of creation is not God at all, and men should worship the creation instead of God, thus turning to Satan as the "god" of this world (2 Cor. 4:3–4).

The Great Scattering

With such a powerful satanic conspiracy developing, the triune God finally would allow it to proceed no further. *"This they begin to do,"* He said, *"and now nothing will be restrained from them, which they have imagined to do"* (Gen. 11:6).

Apparently practically all of Noah's descendants, not just Nimrod and the family of Ham, had joined together in the rebellion. Probably Noah himself and Shem and perhaps a few others refused to join the Babel project (Noah and Shem were still living at the time; Noah lived for 350 years after the Flood and Shem 502 years — see Gen. 9:28; 11:10–11). But practically the entire human family had become subservient to Nimrod in his monstrous scheme.

Satan, behind the scenes, and possibly in direct spirit communication with Nimrod, was undoubtedly instigating and supervising the project. The original evangelical meaning of the star signs gradually was corrupted into the system of astrology and idolatry, persuading men to worship the creation, especially the demonic hosts in the heavens as the creator of all things, instead of the true Creator God. Thus, pagan religion in all its allurements was developed, possibly by means originally of getting men to think that all this was really pleasing to the God of Noah and Shem. But Satan was the father of lies, and this was his scheme for diverting men's thoughts from the Creator to the things of the world, especially the heavenly bodies where the devil and his angels were operating.

God's response, of course, was to force the people to separate from each other by supernaturally implanting in the minds of each family unit a different language. If they could not communicate with each other, they could no longer cooperate with each other in their "one-world" project of rebelling against God and then following their man-made (and devil-inspired) religion. *"The LORD did there confound the language of all the earth: and from thence did the LORD scatter them abroad upon the face of all the earth"* (Gen. 11:9).

This was the beginning of the nations of the earth. God had told them to multiply and fill the earth, and now He forced them to do so, scattering them rapidly into the four corners of the earth. This event resulted in the generation of the 70 original nations, as outlined in Genesis 10 and discussed in chapter IV of this book. The three branches of Noah's family were all scattered, *"divided in their lands: every one after his tongue, after their families, in their nations"* (Gen. 10:5; note also Gen. 10:26, 31, 32).

Some became great nations, not too far from Babel, while others were forced farther and farther away as the tribes competed for the most productive locations, until finally people had settled all over the world, in every continent, proceeding to implement God's primeval mandate first to fill and then to subdue the earth. In the process, however, they largely ignored the fact that this originally had been *God's* dominion mandate, and they were supposed to treat their work and study as a holy stewardship for the glory of God and the benefit of mankind.

In the meantime, as they each finally settled in some location somewhere on the earth, each family group was relatively small and most of their efforts had to be devoted just to their survival, in what could best be described as a "hunting and gathering culture." As the clan grew and as they were able to find suitable metallic ores and building materials, they could develop more complex societies, domesticating animals, and planting and harvesting crops.

Instead of living in caves or simple shelters built of wood and mud, as they necessarily had to do at first, they eventually were able to construct more lasting homes and other buildings in a sort of village economy. Then, with further growth and specialization, they could eventually develop what could be called a true civilization. However, those artifacts excavated by modern archaeologists could easily be misinterpreted as showing primitive humans evolving from savagery to barbarian status and finally to a civilized society over long ages of slow evolution. In reality the true message was one of a small clan gradually becoming able to put into practice skills they already possessed but could not use until more children could grow and suitable materials could be located.

Some groups would be able to develop fairly rapidly. Others, particularly certain disadvantaged or slothful sub-family units (e.g., Neanderthals and other "cavemen") would eventually die out. The ancient Book of Job seems to refer to some of these as still extant in Job's day. *"For want and famine they were solitary; fleeing in to the wilderness in former time desolate and waste, Who cut up mallows by the bushes, and juniper roots for their meat. They were driven forth from among men, (they cried after them as after a thief;) To dwell in the cliffs of the valleys, in caves of the earth, and in the rocks. Among the bushes they brayed; under the nettles they were gathered together. They were children of fools, yea, children of base men: they were viler than the earth"* (Job 30:3–8).

Thus, these early men were not evolving ape-men at all, but degenerate descendants of Noah scattering out from Babel. There may even be a cryptic reference to the judgment at Babel in another statement by Job: *"He removeth away the speech of the trusty, and taketh away the understanding of the ages. . . . He increaseth the nations, and destroyeth them: He enlargeth the nations, and straiteneth them again. He taketh away the heart of the chief of the people of the earth, and causeth them to wander in a wilderness where there is no way"* (Job 12:20–24).

When the tribes had to scatter from Babel, they had to scatter into the wilderness of the post-Flood world. There was "no way" for them to travel — no roads, no caravan routes, no established sea lanes. But they had to go and make their own ways. In some mysterious way, however, they were being directed by God, for it was *"the most High"* who *"divided to the nations their inheritance"* when *"he set the bounds of the people"* (Deut. 32:8).

Many centuries later, the apostle Paul reminded some of the descendants of Japheth there in Athens that it was the Creator God who had made *"all nations of men for to dwell on all the face of the earth, and hath determined the times before appointed, and the bounds of their habitation"* (Acts 17:26).

God seems not only to have determined where each nation should settle but also how long it would last, the duration presumably based on how honestly they proceeded to *"seek the Lord"* (Acts 17:27). It is significant that few, if any, of the 70 original nations named in the Table of Nations have survived as such into the present. There have been many mergers, many divisions, many conquests, etc., so that new nations have been formed over and over again, each surviving for a time. The original languages have proliferated into some 6,600 languages today, scattered through some 200 or more distinct nations. All people today are, nevertheless, descendants of one of the three sons of Noah.

Most of them carried with them some distorted recollection of the story of the great Flood which their grandfathers had told them about. A few kept the remembrance of Babel and the reason for their scattering, but most wanted to forget this traumatic experience. All seemed to retain a vague and somewhat distorted knowledge of God himself as the true sovereign and judge of the world.

However, instead of repenting and turning back to God, most seemed to resent Him more than ever. Instead of renewing their worship of the true Creator, they preferred to keep involved in the new ways of belief and worship taught them by King Nimrod.

Although their languages had all been changed, they still preserved the sensuous religious concepts relayed to them by their former king. The particular names associated with the various stars and the gods (and goddesses) associated with them were different now in each language, but the pantheon was still the same, and the astrological system developed around the signs of the zodiac was still the same. The result was that the pagan religion imparted to the men and women at Babel, though diversifying into different religions in each nation, was still essentially the same everywhere.

This pagan religion, no matter what particular structure it assumed in the practice of each clan, was built around the denial of the Creator as the one true God and ruler of the world. Instead, the world itself, including the stars, was revered as the ultimate reality. The various spirits in the heavens, directed by the great spirit Satan, were identified individually with the many forces and systems in the creation — that is, with the god of the ocean, the goddess of the forests, and so on. The overall system was pantheism, with the creation itself assumed to be the creator of everything in it. This was basically a form of evolutionism, and was manifested in idolatrous polytheism, with the "all-god" made visible and sensual by idols representing the many forces of nature and the spirits supposedly controlling those forces. The system of astrology governed its overall understanding, and spiritism, the practice of receiving guidance from demonic spirits, empowered all its daily activities.

CHAPTER IV

THE TABLE OF NATIONS

T here were no nations as such, of course, when Noah came off the ark after the Flood — only eight people, consisting of Noah, his wife, his three sons and their respective wives. The sons were Shem, Ham, and Japheth, with Japheth probably the oldest and Ham the youngest (Gen. 7:13; 9:23–24; 10:21). These were earth's only inhabitants at the time. The biblical account tells us explicitly that *"by these were the nations divided in the earth after the flood"* and that *"of them was the whole earth overspread"* (Gen. 9:19; 10:32).

The ark, after floating freely over all the mountains of the ancient world for a *"hundred and fifty days,"* finally *"rested . . . upon the mountains of Ararat"* (Gen. 8:3–4), so it was from Ararat (same Hebrew word as "Armenia") that the first inhabitants of the present world emerged. As was confirmed in an ICR computer study,[1] this region is very near the geographical center of the earth's land surfaces above sea level, so the landing site was an ideal location from which Noah's descendants could proceed to *"overspread"* the earth. This surely was an evidence of God's providence.

With no more violence filling the world, and with men and women still living hundreds of years, the human population could again increase rapidly. Noah soon had at least 16 named grandsons and (although not named) probably about the same number of granddaughters. This

---

1 Andrew Woods and Henry Morris, *The Center of the Earth* (San Diego, CA: Institute for Creation Research, 1973).

information is obtained from Genesis 10, popularly known now as the "Table of Nations." It is possible that this entire list of names was originally a family genealogical chart kept by Shem, who also included the names of a number of Noah's great grandchildren, especially those in his own (i.e., Shem's family). See Genesis 11:10 (*"these are the generations of Shem"*), which seems to be a sort of signature to the record of Genesis 10:2–11:9.

Noah's Prophecy Concerning His Sons

Why would Shem be the one to keep this record? The important event narrated in Genesis 9:20–27 seems to suggest the reason. This event occurred sometime after the family had descended from the ark there on its mountain and established homes for the four families. Enough time had elapsed for Noah to have produced wine from his vineyard and all three of Noah's sons to have developed families of their own (note the reference to Ham's youngest son, Canaan, in Genesis 9:22).

One day, unfortunately, Noah became drunk from his wine and lay asleep uncovered in his tent. His youngest son, Ham, *"saw"* him, presumably staring in a leering and disrespectful way. When he told his brothers, they refused to look at Noah, but covered him with all due care and respect for their father.

When Noah learned what had happened, it became clear to him that the characteristics he had seen developing in his three sons would in significant measure be transmitted genetically to their descendants. In a general way (though with due allowance for many individual exceptions), the nations descending from each one of them would tend to manifest the characteristics of their respective fathers.

But this was not just Noah's opinion. He proceeded to utter a remarkable prophecy, a prophecy no doubt inspired by God (who could also see these tendencies already in the families of the three sons). Here is the prophecy:

> *Cursed be Canaan; a servant of servants shall he be unto his brethren. . . . Blessed be the Lord God of Shem; and Canaan shall be his servant. God shall enlarge Japheth, and he shall dwell in the tents of Shem: and Canaan shall be his servant* (Gen. 9:25–27).

We need to understand, of course, that this was not just a petulant expostulation on Noah's part, but rather a divine prophecy given by God and based on the fundamental characters of the three sons that had just been exposed by this unexpected family crisis. It did not apply directly to the three men themselves (Canaan never became a servant to his two uncles, and Japheth never moved in with Shem), but rather to the nations that would come from them.

The key seems to be the tripartite nature of man. That is, every person has a physical component, a mental component, and a spiritual component to his nature. Furthermore, one of these components tends to dominate the other two. Some tend to be dominated by physical interests — athletes, soldiers, machinists, etc. Others are primarily intellectual in their interests and abilities, such as scientists, accountants, journalists, and the like. Some are gifted and motivated more by spiritual attributes, including pastors, teachers, and religious authors. Many seem to be fairly balanced in terms of all three components, but inevitably one of the three tends to outweigh the others at least to some degree.

It is the same way with nations. Physical interests largely characterize some peoples, intellectual pursuits some, and spiritual motivations others. In a very general sense (with exceptions, of course) these three characteristics have tended to dominate in Hamitic, Japhetic, and Shemitic nations, respectively. This was probably the main thrust of Noah's prophecy.

Thus, Shem would be the son through whom the knowledge of God and His will would be transmitted to future generations. Japheth would be *"enlarged"* — not in the sense of geographical territory, but intellectual achievements. Ham (addressed through his youngest son, Canaan, since he was Noah's youngest son) would be servant to the others in the sense that he would provide the material foundations upon which the intellectual and spiritual contributions of the others could be built and implemented. This was presumably considered a *"curse,"* because Ham's work would be more directly associated than the others with *"the ground which the"Lord hath cursed"* (Gen. 5:29).

The word *"servant"* conveys the idea of "steward," rather than "slave," in its Hebrew usage. Both Japheth and Shem were servants of God in this sense, and Ham was to be a servant to these two servants

— that is, he would be a steward providing physical support to enable God's intellectual and spiritual stewards to function effectively. The idea of slavery is not the intended meaning of *"servant of servants."* The Hamitic nations and even some of the Canaanites (e.g., the Hittites) actually became great empires for a time. In another sense, *"servant of servants"* could be understand as "extraordinary servant," for Hamitic nations (Sumeria, Phoenicia, Egypt, and others) have indeed made many essential contributions to the basic material life of mankind.

The Japhetic nations (Greece, Germany, England, etc.) have been preeminent in scientific and philosophical contributions to society, and it is, of course, the Semitic nations — especially Israel, but also the Arabic peoples — through whom a monotheistic faith in one Creator God has been transmitted. The Japhethites have also, as Noah prophesied, eventually come to dwell spiritually under the religious tent built by the Shemites.

These observations concerning the relative character and contributions of the three streams of nations have been discussed more fully by Dr. Arthur Custance.[2] For now, we wish to turn to the actual origin of the individual nations.

The Table of Nations

Genesis chapter 10 is a remarkable document, unique among the writings of the ancient world. There is nothing comparable to it from Greece or Egypt or any other early nation. Premier archaeologist William F. Albright once called it "an astonishingly accurate document" and noted that it "stands absolutely alone in ancient literature, without a remote parallel, even among the Greeks. . . ."[3] As noted above, it probably was originally written as a sort of family tree document by Shem, who lived for 502 years after the Flood, well past the time of the dispersion at Babel, and who could certainly have kept up with the names and relationships of all the men listed in the table. Shem and his two brothers had apparently been co-authors of the account of the Flood itself (Genesis 6:9–10:1), and had separated soon after Noah's

---

2 Arthur Custance, *Noah's Three Sons* (Grand Rapids, MI: Zodervan Publishing Co.).

3 William F. Albright, *Recent Discoveries in Bible Lands* (New York, NY: Funk and Wagnall's Co., 1936), p. 25. Dr. Albright had been director of the American School of Oriental Research in Jerusalem.

disquieting prophecy, with Shem taking over the sole responsibility of record-keeping thereafter.

There are 70 names listed in the table: 14, 30, and 26 in the families of Japheth, Ham, and Shem, respectively, and presumably each of them established what was considered a "nation," although several may never have become more than small city-states, a type of political entity which was common in the ancient world. Many, of course, did become great nations, as discussed below.

In any case, the number 70 seems intriguingly significant in light of the statement in the farewell song of Moses in Deuteronomy 32:7–8 almost a thousand years later.

> *Remember the days of old, consider the years of many generations: ask thy father, and he will shew thee; thy elders, and they will tell thee. When the Most High divided to the nations their inheritance, when he separated the sons of Adam, he set the bounds of the people according to the number of the children of Israel.*

The *"number of the children of Israel"* seems to refer to the number of Jacob's (that is, Israel's) children that went with him into Egypt: *". . . all the souls of the house of Jacob, which came into Egypt, were threescore and ten"* (Gen. 46:27).

Assuming there were indeed just 70 original nations (this would evidently be at the time of their dispersion at Babel), and recognizing that God, by His foreknowledge, would know that there would be 70 original *"children of Israel,"* on just what basis would He give each nation its *"inheritance"* and set their boundaries? At present the relationship is elusive, perhaps being among the *"secret things"* which God has not revealed (Deut. 29:29). There must be some connection, however, as God is not capricious and He somehow ordained it so.

There is also a very strategic verse in the New Testament having to do with these boundaries of the nations. This was in Paul's important address to the Athenian philosophers in the great nation of Greece.

> *God that made the world and all things therein, seeing that he is Lord of heaven and earth, dwelleth not in temples made with hands; Neither is worshipped with men's hands, as though he needeth any thing, seeing he giveth to all life, and breath, and all*

things; And hath made of one blood all nations of men for to dwell on all the face of the earth, and hath determined the times before appointed, and the bounds of their habitation (Acts 17:24–26).

This verse parallels in a very real way the similar passage in Moses' song, as cited above (Deut. 32:8), although it was written over a thousand years after Moses and over two thousand years since Shem wrote down his Table of Nations, and it also relates to that great event when God established the nations.

We learn from Paul that God established boundaries for the nations, not only geographically but also chronologically. As it has turned out historically, therefore, nations rise and nations fall. Very few of the nations in the Table of Nations, for example, are still nations. New nations take over the boundaries originally deeded by God to nations now gone and some even forgotten. Like the 70 original children of Israel, who all have died individually but who have proliferated nationally into many millions of other Israelites throughout history, so the 70 original nations have largely vanished from the earth, but have been succeeded by many other nations that took over their respective inheritances.

In some essentially inscrutable way, all these national successions have been *"determined"* by God, and He has planned it all from the beginning. *"Known unto God are all his works from the beginning of the world"* (Acts 15:18).

On what basis has God determined when nations raised up by Him were finally to be allowed to fall and perish from the earth? This also was clarified by Paul as he addressed the philosophers. The very purpose of the various nations, he said, was *"that they should seek the Lord, if haply they might feel after him, and find him, though he be not far from every one of us: For in him we live, and move, and have our being"* (Acts 17:27–28).

It is sad to realize, as we try to identify the 70 original nations in Genesis 10, that most of them did indeed reject God, even though He was not very far from every one of them. After all, they were only a little over a century removed from the judgment of the Flood. In fact, Noah and Shem were still living and, no doubt, doing what they could to keep them from their imminent apostasy.

But down they went, and so did most of those who succeeded them. The present nations of the world are their genetic and spiritual heirs, and they, also, are facing imminent judgment.

Right now, however, we need to identify as well as we can these original nations. Just before they became nations, of course, they all spoke the same language, and so, in effect, constituted one united nation, the same as in the antediluvian world. However, they soon became united against God, rebelling against Him at Babel. Shem also has recorded that event in Genesis 11, in order to explain the origin of the nations as he had tabulated them in Genesis 10, *"after their families, after their tongues, in their lands, after their nations"* (Gen. 10:31).

The Original Japhetic Nations

The eldest son of Noah was Japheth, and his seven sons are recorded as *"Gomer, and Magog, and Madai, and Javan, and Tubal, and Meshech, and Tiras"* (Gen. 10:2). That these moved north and west from Ararat (and Babel) in most cases is almost indisputable. Japheth himself is often associated with the Iapeti, reputed to be the ancestors of the Greeks. The same name is given as an ancestor of the Aryans, in India. In fact, the Japhethites as a whole might well be the group of peoples whom secular ethnologists have called Indo-Europeans.

Gomer is identified by the Greek historian Herodotus with the Cimmerians, a name still surviving in the region now known as Crimea. Some of these people migrated farther west, possibly into Germany and even Cambria (Wales). Magog seems to mean "the place of Gog," where Gog is possibly the country still called Georgia, one of the former Soviet republics. Madai is agreed by all historians to be the ancestor of the Medes, and Javan is universally identified with the Ionians, or Greeks. The word occurs fairly often in the Old Testament, and is often even translated as "Greece."

Tubal and Meschech are found together in a number of other Old Testament passages, and were apparently located in what is now southern Russia. The names seem rather definitely to be preserved today in the two key Russian cities of Tobolsk and Moscow, the latter associated with the Muskovites. Japheth's seventh son, Tiras, was very likely ancestor of the Thracians and/or, possibly, the Etruscans.

Seven grandsons of Japheth are also listed in the Table. *"And the sons of Gomer; Ashkenaz, and Riphath, and Togarmah. And the sons of Javan; Elishah, and Tarshish, Kittim, and Dodanim"* (Gen. 10:3–4). These seem to be two sons of Japheth with whom Shem had maintained contact long enough to know the names of their children.

The name Ashkenaz has long been associated with the German Jews, though the association has been disputed. Some have suggested a connection to the names Scandia and Saxony. The archaeologist William Albright has found good reason to connect it with the Scythians, the latter people being also associated by Josephus, the Jewish historian, with the Magogites.

The name Riphath is connected by Josephus with the Paphlagonians. The name may also be the source of the names Carpathia, and even Europe. Togarmah, along with his father, Gomer, is connected with Germany in the Jewish Targums. It may also be that Togarmah is the source of the name Armenia or even Turkey.

Elishah is preserved today through the name Hellas (Hellespont, Hellenists), the same nation as Greece. The Iliad apparently mentions them as the Eilesians.

Tarshish is a name used frequently in the Bible in reference to a wide-ranging seafaring people. They seem occasionally to be involved with the Phoenicians and their city of Carthage in North Africa, although the latter were of Hamite origin. Many believe the name Tartessus in Spain refers to Tarshish.

Kittim is another name for Cyprus. The name Ma-Kittim ("land of Kittim") is possibly preserved as Macedonia. Dodanim is probably the same as Rodanim. The names are probably found today in the names Dardanelles and Rhodes.

> *By these were the isles* [or, preferably, seacoasts] *of the Gentiles divided in their lands; every one after his tongue* [therefore, after Babel's dispersion], *after their families, in their nations* (Gen. 10:5).

The First Shemite Nations

Interestingly, Shem, who probably was the original author of the Table of Nations, took pains to call himself *"the father of all the children of Eber"* (Gen. 10:21), although Eber was just one of his descendants, actually his great grandson (Shem to Arphaxad to Salah to Eber — verse 24). Eber is the source of the term "Hebrew," so the latter term would technically apply not only to Israelites but all others descended from Eber. The latter was apparently an important king when Shem was writing — in fact, he may have been the king of Ebla, an important archaeological site in northern Syria. That king, according to the famous Ebla tablets discovered there, was named "Ebrim," and could well have been the same man.

In any case, Shem was 201 years old when Eber fathered Peleg. This was 101 years after the flood, assuming no gaps in the genealogies (compare Gen. 11:10, 12, 14, 16), and it may be that the name Peleg was given him by Eber because *"in his days was the earth divided"* (Gen. 10:25). This division has been understood by some as an actual splitting apart of the one continental landmass, but in the context of Shem's own writings it most likely refers to the "dividing" of the post-diluvian population at the time of their rebellion at Babel under Nimrod.

The *"children of Eber,"* of course, eventually included Terah and Abram, as well as Peleg. It was evidently Terah to whom Shem gave the task of continuing to record the history of the chosen line (compare Gen. 11:10 and 11:27), and Abram which God called to found his chosen nation. Shem actually lived 75 more years after Terah died, and even outlived Abraham, being 602 years old when he finally died (Gen. 11:10–11). As many writers have noted, the longevity of people began an exponential decline after the Flood, so Shem outlived many of his descendants.

Whatever the reason may be, most of the Shemitic (or Semitic, if preferred) "nations" listed by Shem in his Table of Nations turned out to be rather short-lived city-states instead of enduring nations. Shem called them *"nations"* but this was probably because after Babel each of the *"families"* occupied separate *"lands"* and all spoke distinctive *"tongues"* (Gen. 10:31).

Several tribes, however, did develop into important long-lasting nations. Shem's own children were *"Elam and Asshur, and Arphaxad, and Lud and Aram"* (Gen. 10:22), and each of these turned out to be quite significant as Semitic nations.

Elam was the ancestor of the Elamites, who later merged with the Medes (descendants of Madai, a Japhethite) to form the great

Medo-Persian empire. Asshur gave his name to the Assyrians, although his city on the Tigris River was eventually conquered by Nimrod and his Sumerians (Gen. 10:11).

Lud was said by Josephus to be the ancestor of the Lydians. Arphaxad, of course, was the ancestor of Eber and, therefore, also of Ishmael, progenitor of the Arabic people, and Abraham, from whom came the elect nation Israel.

Aram was the father of the Aramaeans, later better known as Syrians, prominent throughout the biblical record. In fact, the Aramaic language became for a time almost a world language. Even some parts of the Old Testament were written in Aramaic, and the common people of Jesus' day often used Aramaic in speaking.

As far as the other names in Shem's portion of the table are concerned, most expositors believe that they largely settled in southern and eastern Arabia, but the evidence is minimal. In any case, we have to assume that later nations eventually displaced and replaced them.

The Earliest Hamitic Nations

The nations descended from Ham have been introduced last in this chapter (not in Gen. 10, but in this discussion here), because of the key role played by Ham's grandson, Nimrod, in the formation of the first nations. The rebellion led by Nimrod at Babel provoked the decision by God to enforce separation of the early families into distinct nations with distinct languages.

At that particular time — about 101 years after the Flood if there are no gaps in the genealogies recorded in Genesis 11 — all the descendants of Noah (or nearly all; one would assume that Shem and Japheth themselves either remained near Noah or at least separated from Ham's family) had stayed together, eventually settling in Shinar (probably equivalent to Sumer) and building the city of Babel. In addition, they all still spoke the same language, presumably the same as Adam's original language or some modification thereof.

Having described the three divisions of mankind in his Table of Nations in Genesis 10, Shem evidently felt constrained to explain how this division came about. This he proceeded to do in Genesis 11:1–10, finally closing his narrative with his signature statement: *"These are the generations of Shem"* (Gen. 11:10).

He introduced Nimrod in Genesis 10:8 as *"a mighty one in the earth,"* but also as the youngest son of Cush, who was the eldest son of Ham. The four sons of Ham were *"Cush, and Mizraim, and Phut, and Canaan"* (Gen. 10:6), all four of whom founded important nations. Since the meaning of the name Nimrod is probably "Let us rebel" (the Hebrew word for "rebel" is *marad*), we can assume that, by the time of the birth of his own youngest son, Cush had become so resentful of God's association of the "curse" with his father's family in Noah's prophecy that he decided they should rebel against that action, and so proceeded to name and train his son Nimrod with that purpose in mind.

In any case, Nimrod became the first and definitive king of Babel, the city founded by Noah's descendants in the land of Shinar (known to modern archaeologists, with its surrounding region, as Sumeria, the first great empire in world history). There he led the great rebellion that resulted in God's judgment of the confusion of languages and worldwide dispersion of the nations.

After the dispersion, Nimrod remained as king in Sumeria for a long time (probably much later, long after the dispersion), and it did indeed become a great empire (though utterly pagan) on its own. He later conquered Assyria (originally founded by the Semite Asshur — Gen. 10:22) and its capital Nineveh, so that more than 1,200 years later, the latter was still called *"the land of Nimrod"* (Mic. 5:6).

Nimrod's father, Cush, no doubt supported his son in the tower episode at Babel, and the rebellion in general, but was forced to leave along with all the other families there when God scattered them abroad. "Cush" is usually translated in the Bible as "Ethiopia," which apparently is the land eventually settled by the Cushites (or "Kashi," as they are called in the Tel El Amarna tablets). It is interesting also to note that the Cushites seem first to have settled in southern Arabia, just across the Red Sea from Ethiopia, for that area was also known as Cush for a considerable length of time. Among Cush's sons of lesser influence (Seba, Havilah, Sabtah, Raamah, Sabtechah, Sheba, and Dedan — verse 7), the very limited evidence points also to southwestern Arabia as their home after Babel.

The other three sons of Ham (Mizraim, Phut, Canaan) were also very important in terms of the nations established by them after Babel. Mizraim was the founder of the great nation of Egypt; in fact, the name "Egypt," which occurs hundreds of times in the Old Testament, is actually translated from "Mizraim," evidently the name of its first king. Egypt is also called "the land of Ham" several times in the Bible, suggesting that Ham also was still living at the time of the dispersion and migrated to Egypt along with his son Mizraim.

The sons of Mizraim were *"Ludim, and Anamim, and Lehabim, and Naphtihim, And Pathrusian, and Casluhim, (out of whom came Philistim) and Caphtorim"* (Gen. 10:13–14).

Most of these "nations" have not been identified in secular history. However, the Philistines (whose name is the source of the modern name, Palestine) have also been associated in the Bible with the Caphtorim (Amos 9:7), and Caphtor is the same as Crete in secular history.

The Pathrusim are identified with Pathros, which was Upper Egypt in ancient times. There is also a possibility that the Lehabim could be the same as Libya.

Phut, the third son of Ham, is not as clearly identified as Mizraim, but the weight of evidence would indicate probably that he migrated farther west than Mizraim, and settled in the area now known as Libya. Another suggestion has been that Phut (or Put) was in what is now called Somaliland, adjacent to Ethiopia.

The youngest son, Canaan, and his descendants settled mostly in what later became Israel's "promised land," south of Syria, northeast of Egypt and west of Arabia. There, Canaan became the ancestor of the Phoenicians (Sidon was his firstborn, whose city became the chief city, along with Tyre of that leading nautical kingdom of the ancient world). He also fathered the Hittites (descendants of Heth, his second son), then the Jebusites, Amorites, Girgasites, Hivites, Arkites, Sinites, Arvadites, Zemarites, and Hamathites — most of them collectively known to Moses and Joshua later as the Canaanites.

Of these, the Hitties and Sinites are of special interest. The Hittites actually became an empire of considerable significance, centered primarily in Turkey, although they also had an important contingent in Canaan. Furthermore, some scholars have noted certain resemblances between their monuments and those of the earliest pioneers who migrated east from Ararat and Babel into Asia, especially the Chinese.

Interestingly, the name "Cathay" (referring to China) seems to have certain linguistic affinity with "Khittae," which is the term identifying the Hittites in the ancient monuments. Shem's record also notes that later *"the families of the Canaanites spread abroad"* (Gen. 10:18).

This suggests the intriguing possibility that certain groups of Canaanites (notably the Hittites and perhaps also the Sinites, whose very name suggests China) may have spread over into the great Asian continent as well. The record does say that of the three sons of Noah *"was the whole earth overspread"* (Gen. 9:19; see also Gen. 10:32).

Another interesting question concerning the Table of Nations would have to do with the many nations of sub-Saharan Africa. The Hamites clearly settled Egypt and Ethiopia, and probably Libya, so the presumption would be that these nations or others related to the Hamites eventually colonized the other regions of Africa as well.

These suggestions concerning Asia and Africa are, of course, very tentative, since these particular regions are not mentioned directly in the Table of Nations.

The same is true, of course, of the nations in the two American continents. The present American nations were founded by Japhethite peoples from Europe. However, the Indian tribes who had settled there earlier apparently migrated there mostly from Asia, and the same is true of the island nations in the Pacific. All of these, therefore, seem likely to have come from the same original peoples as did the Chinese and other Asian nations soon after the dispersion at Babel.

It is remarkable that, even though many of the names in the Table of Nations cannot now be identified with nations known in ancient secular history, many of these *can* be so recognized. As Dr. Albright said, it is an "astonishingly accurate document."

Very few nations last a long time, of course. Nations rise and nations fall. One nation succeeds another in a given region, and then still another, and this process has been going on for centuries. All of this is taking place within the providence of God (and perhaps often by His direct intervention). As both Moses and Paul have reminded us (Deut. 32:8; Acts 17:24–26), the times and boundaries of the nations have been determined somehow by God, largely in reference to their individual faithfulness and effectiveness in carrying out His will for the nation.

CHAPTER V

GOD'S APPOINTED BOUNDS AND TIMES

Teachers of Bible prophecy frequently refer to a coming time of apostasy near the end of the age. Actually, in the course of Christian history there have been many times of great apostasy, when professing Christians in large numbers have fallen away from the faith in Christ they had once professed.

But the greatest apostasy of all occurred long ago, when practically the entire world renounced the true God and espoused faith in a false God. The event to which we refer is the rebellion against God led by Nimrod at Babel, as discussed in the foregoing chapter.

The entire antediluvian world had been inundated by the Flood and its population destroyed, except for eight men and women saved on Noah's ark. For some little time, as the post-Flood population grew, all people living (including even Ham and his sons, no doubt) were aware of the purpose of the Flood and the saving work of God with respect to its survivors. They all knew the Lord and His mighty power and purposes for His creation.

But then came the subversive acts of Nimrod and possibly of Cush, his father, and soon their entire generation was led astray. Even after the judgment on Babel and the resulting worldwide dispersion, the people did not repent, but continued in their apostasy. And, as always, religious apostasy soon led to moral degeneration.

This situation is recounted in the burning words of Paul's epistle to the Romans.

> *When they knew God, they glorified him not as God, neither were thankful; but became vain in their imaginations, and their foolish heart was darkened. Professing themselves to be wise, they became fools, And changed the glory of the uncorruptible God into an image made like to corruptible man, and to birds, and fourfooted beasts, and creeping things* (Rom. 1:21–23).

Being "wise" in their own foolishness, they wanted to make a name for themselves instead of serving the God who had saved them from the terrible fate of the antediluvians. This resulted, as noted in the preceding chapter, in the worship of the host of heaven and the created universe instead of the Creator of the universe. This soon led to astrology and gross idolatry in their religious interests.

> *Wherefore God also gave them up to uncleanness through the lusts of their own hearts, to dishonour their own bodies between themselves: Who changed the truth of God into a lie, and worshipped and served the creature more than the Creator, who is blessed for ever. Amen* (Rom. 1:24–25).

Spiritual apostasy inevitably leads to moral degradation. They had known the true God, but in only a few generations after the Flood, they had rebelled against Him and proceeded to worship the forces of nature, personified as various gods and goddesses. In reality they were following and worshipping the wicked spirits led by Satan. Such descent into evolutionary pantheistic paganism was soon followed (as it always is) by gross immorality when God *"gives them up."*

> *For this cause, God gave them up unto vile affections: for even their women did change the natural use into that which is against nature: And likewise also the men, leaving the natural use of the woman, burned in their lust one toward another; men with men working that which is unseemly, and receiving in themselves that recompence of their error which was meet* (Rom. 1:26–27).

Forgetting altogether the divine purpose of marriage (one man and one woman united together for life, as prescribed in Gen. 1:26–28 and Gen. 2:18, 22–24) and its primary purpose (that of filling the earth and caring for it as a God-given stewardship), both men and women proceeded to corrupt the wonderful procreative process entrusted to them by God. Not only did they ignore the principle of monogamy and the sacred ritual of marriage, but even left the principle of heterosexuality, indulging in the gross perversions of homosexuality and lesbianism. These, indeed, became widespread in the ancient world and are now even inflaming the "Christianized" modern world.

Such flagrant widespread immorality inevitably leads to all sorts of wicked and even criminal activity. It was so then, and so it is today.

> *And even as they did not like to retain God in their knowledge, God gave them over to a reprobate mind, to do those things which are not convenient; Being filled with all unrighteousness, wickedness, covetousness; maliciousness; full of envy, murder, debate, deceit, malignity, whisperers, Backbiters, haters of God, despiteful, proud, boasters, inventors of evil things, disobedient to parents, Without understanding, covenant breakers, without natural affection, implacable, unmerciful: Who knowing the judgment of God, that they which commit such things are worthy of death, not only do the same, but have pleasure in them that do them* (Rom. 1:28–32).

This terrible catalogue of evil soon became a fit description of the ancient pagan world, especially those of its leaders. No wonder God gave them up! The fearful aspect of all this, of course, is that it is becoming more and more a description of the modern world, even among those nations that profess Christianity.

That the above narrative was primarily referring to the ancient, post-diluvian world, however, is obvious from its introductory words — *"When they knew God"* (Rom. 1:21) — because that was the only time in post-diluvian world history when it could be said that the world as a whole knew God. Thus, the terrible description of what happened to that world apparently applied to *all* of these nations that were formed following the dispersion at Babel. As we shall discuss in the next chapter, that global apostasy was the reason God had to form a new nation, Israel, through Abraham.

The Appointed Bounds and Times

There is no need to review the secular records of these ancient nations individually, since God's record in Romans 1 is and should be definitive. *All* of them, without exception, seem not only to have rejected God but then also to have descended into gross wickedness. Even though they did not yet have a written revelation of God's law, they all did have God's moral *"law written in their hearts, their conscience also bearing witness"* (Rom. 2:15), so they did know their actions were grossly wrong in God's economy. The worst sin of all, of course, was rejecting God in favor of Nimrod and the host of heaven, and therefore also ignoring God's original institution of monogamous marriage and its purpose of filling the earth and exercising stewardship over it.

Nevertheless, God was patient and long-suffering, allowing each nation a time and place to function as a nation under God, to *"seek the Lord, if haply they might feel after him, and find him, though he be not far from every one of us"* (Acts 17:27).

For this purpose, He guided each nation's founders into the foreordained *"bounds of their habitation,"* and allowed them *"the time before appointed"* to carry out their respective parts in His original plan (Acts 17:26). Thus, Mizraim settled in North Africa, Cush in Ethiopia, Javan in what would become Greece, Elam in the future Persia, Aram to the eastern shore of the Mediterranean, and so on. There each nation, with its own divinely imparted language, proceeded to develop its own culture and civilization.

Asshur, a son of Shem, settled north of Babel, giving his name to what would become the nation of Assyria. However, Nimrod, who apparently remained at Babel, later conquered that region also, and built the great city of Nineveh, its capital (Gen. 10:11). Micah 5:6 actually calls Assyria the *"land of Nimrod."* It was in the Assyro-Babylonia region — in particular its great southern city of Ur — where Terah lived. Terah was a descendant of Shem through Shem's son Arphaxad. The latter was still living during Terah's lifetime and presumably had preserved Shem's spiritual legacy in some measure down to Terah and finally to Terah's son Abraham, assuming there are no gaps in the genealogies of Genesis 11:10–26; 25:7.

For that matter, even the patriarch Noah did not finally die until Abraham was 58 years old. Many Bible students have noted, of course, that longevity was only gradually decreasing from its pre-Flood average of over 900 years, eventually declining to the normative average of about 70 by the time of Moses. This was a key factor in the rapid development of a rather large world population by the time of Abraham, who lived until just 467 years after the great Flood (again assuming no genealogical gaps). Very reasonable assumptions applied to population growth equations show that there could easily have been several million people in the world before Abraham died. If there were actually one or more gaps in these genealogies, the population by Abraham's time would be even larger, of course.

As noted before, most or all of the original nations formed at Babel are now gone, although their descendants are, of course, still here under various other identities. Nations come and go, as ordained by God. The criteria by which God has determined *"the times before appointed"* for each in turn probably have been their honesty, efficiency, and perseverance in two main responsibilities: (1) seeking and finding God, as stressed by Paul at Athens (Acts 17:27); and (2) carrying out, either consciously or unknowingly, the primeval dominion mandate (Gen. 1:26–28). Those nations which were effectively fulfilling one or both of these criteria seem to have been the ones that survived the longest, at least as a rule. Those that failed on both counts have vanished as independent nations, replaced by others arising out of their remnants in many cases.

The first great empires, for example, were Sumeria and Egypt. Both contributed much to the advance of civilization (thus unintentionally advancing the goals of the dominion mandate), but eventually were terminated because of failing in their search for God (remember that the present country called Egypt is altogether different in ethnicity and character from the first Egypt). There is still a small population of Coptics (probably descendants of the ancient Egyptians), but Arabs dominate the population there today.

Sumeria was equivalent to the land of Shinar, essentially synonymous with Babylonia, or Mesopotamia. Actually several early kingdoms or city-states were important in this region — Accad, Sumeria, Uruk, Amorites, Aram, Assyria, Babylonia, Chaldea, Ur, etc. — frequently at war with each other but all profoundly influenced by Nimrod and his original kingdom at Babel. Assyria and Babylonia were the most powerful of all these kingdoms of Mesopotamia (the "land between the rivers," the Tigris and Euphrates).

One should remember that most of what we know about these kingdoms, especially their early histories, comes from archaeology, not from written histories. Thousands of clay tablets have been unearthed, and attempts made to deduce their histories from inscriptions (often in cuneiform) on these tablets and also on the occasional larger monuments that have been discovered. But these are incomplete and difficult to interpret, with the result that many different hypotheses have been proposed and argued. Unfortunately, most of the currently practicing archaeologists do not believe in biblical accuracy and many of their ideas conflict with the biblical records.

On the other hand, there are a few highly competent archaeologists who *do* believe the biblical records (in Gen. 10, etc.), and *they* believe that archaeology fully supports the Bible. Consequently, in this book, the accounts in Scripture of Babylon, Assyria, and these other ancient nations are taken as correct even when they seem to disagree with various archaeologists.

As noted before, most of these nations have now been replaced by others in the region, so that their *"times before appointed"* by God are past. Many did contribute significantly to the advance of technology and other aspects of God's dominion mandate and so were allowed to endure for a time, even though they rarely sought the true God, being firmly committed to paganism and the worship of false gods, along with the utterly immoral and ungodly life styles which such heathen worship had engendered.

That God was concerned with this situation and would not allow the nations unlimited time is evident from various passages. For example, the Amorites were a strong and influential people for a long time. The famous Hammurabi, who produced a significant legal code while ruling as an early king of Babylon, was an Amorite.

The Amorites are first mentioned in the Bible as a Canaanite tribe (Gen. 10:16), and later references seem to imply that they were the most prominent and powerful of these tribes during the times of Abraham, even until their final conquest by Moses and Joshua. When God promised the land of Canaan to Abraham, He said that his descendants would first have to live in another land for a long time, *"for the iniquity of the Amorites is not yet full"* (Gen. 15:16). That is, the time allowed to them for the accomplishment of God's commission to them had not yet been exhausted. Later, however, their iniquity was full and their time was up. God gave Moses and Joshua the command to conquer the promised land which had heretofore (and long afterward) been regarded as mainly *"the land of the Amorite"* (Amos 2:10).

This principle of an appointed time for each nation, based on their adherence (or lack thereof) to the will and purposes of God, stated clearly with respect to the Amorites, by implication can be assumed to have applied to other nations as well.

God's dealing with the Assyrian nation is very instructive. Originally founded by Asshur, a son of Shem, it was later conquered by Nimrod. With its capital at Nineveh, it eventually developed into a great empire, but its wickedness and its vicious cruelty toward its defeated foes became notorious. The unique mission of the prophet Jonah, sent by God to preach to the people of Nineveh, illustrates the truth that God has never lost His concern for the Gentile nations, even such a licentious nation as Assyria.

Remarkably, the Assyrian capital did repent and turn back to the true God at Jonah's preaching (Jonah 3:10), so that the city was spared its threatened destruction for a time. However, after only two or three more generations, the Assyrians returned to their evil ways, and this time another prophet, Nahum, proclaimed their imminent and final defeat (Nah. 3:18–19). Indeed, Assyria was soon devastated by a combined force of Babylonians, Medians, and Scythians, under the command of Nebuchadnezzar, who soon became king of Babylon.

Babylon then, for a time was the greatest empire in the world, but it also was eventually removed by God during the reign of Belshazzar. The prophet Daniel records how God sent a hand to write on the wall of the king's banquet chamber that *his* kingdom's time was finished and would be given to the Medo-Persian empire (see Dan. 5). The Babylonians had enjoyed a long period of influence in the world, and had even been used as God's sword to judge His people in Judah, taking them into captivity, but their appointed time had finally ended also.

The famous image of Nebuchadnezzar's dream (see Dan. 2) had been interpreted by Daniel to mean that four great empires would dominate future world history, the first being Babylon itself. The other three, as practically all Bible expositors agree, turned out to be Persia, Greece, and Rome, in that order. Each of these endured for centuries as the most important nation in the world, but each eventually fell. Each played a key role in the plan of God, contributing significantly (though unknowingly) in carrying forward the dominion mandate and also in God's spiritual program.

Persia, for example, kept the chosen nation, Israel, from extinction and also made it possible for the Jewish temple, as well as the city of Jerusalem itself, to be rebuilt after the captivity and exile of Judah.

Greece provided the language of the New Testament, as well as being the nation where most of the early churches were established. Rome, under its third-century emperor Constantine, was the first nation to provide official recognition to the God of the Bible as the one true God of creation, and the various European nations that developed out of the Roman empire later did the same.

This two-fold contribution of Greece and Rome (technological and spiritual) may be the reason why Greece and Rome still are allowed to continue today as viable nations, though not in their original structure. Both Italy and Greece, as well as the other nations of Europe in later years, have deteriorated grievously in both spirituality and morality, though they still officially, as nations, acknowledge God. They still contribute effectively in science and technology and other areas, but real leadership in terms of the dominion mandate seems to have moved westward in the same degree as spiritual leadership. England and America, in particular, have been the nations most effective during the past four centuries both in "subduing" the earth and in acknowledging and proclaiming the true God. How long will be the duration of their times as appointed by God remains for the future to reveal. England has already declined far from its former empire status.

Before discussing the present nations, however, we should note that God has maintained the same criteria in past ages for the smaller nations as well as for the greater. They also have come and gone, one after another. The prophets of the Old Testament have noted God's particular dealings with many of them, especially those that had been special enemies of God's chosen nation. As will be discussed later, God had set one other very specific criterion for dealing with the nations when He called Abraham to establish a new nation that would recognize and honor only one God, the God of creation, repudiating all the other false gods being promoted by the satanic powers in the heavens. God had made the following unconditional promise to Abraham: *"I will make of thee a great nation, and I will bless thee, and make thy name great; and thou shalt be a blessing: And I will bless them that bless thee, and curse him that curseth thee: and in thee shall all families of the earth be blessed"* (Gen. 12:2–3).

Consider the fate of some of those nations that opposed Israel. (These same nations had also rejected God in favor of one or more pagan gods, and also had contributed little toward fulfilling the dominion mandate.)

Take the nations of Moab and Ammon, both descendants of the incestuous relations of Abraham's nephew Lot with Lot's two daughters. *"Moab shall be destroyed from being a people, because he hath magnified himself against the LORD"* (Jer. 48:42). *"Therefore, as I live, saith the LORD of hosts, the God of Israel, Surely Moab shall be as Sodom, and the children of Ammon as Gomorrah . . . a perpetual desolation . . ."* (Zeph. 2:9).

Edom also, the nation descended from Esau, was an inveterate enemy of Israel and thoroughly licentious and idolatrous. God finally had to judge the Edomites too, and this was the entire burden of Obadiah's prophetic message. *"The house of Esau* [shall be] *for stubble . . . and there shall not be any remaining of the house of Esau: for the LORD hath spoken it"* (Obad. 1:18).

Similar judgment was pronounced on Philistia: *"Woe unto the inhabitants of the sea coast . . . O Canaan, the land of the Philistines, I will even destroy thee"* (Zeph. 2:5).

The Phoenicians, especially through their great city of Tyre, made great contributions to the world in navigation and linguistics, but were perennially worshipers of false gods, so their time eventually came also. Note the extensive description of her coming demise in Ezekiel 26, 27, and 28.

There were a few powerful nations that were the subject of similar prophecies of judgment, but which actually still survive even today (e.g., Egypt, Ethiopia, Syria). The key to God's long patience in these cases may be because each of them were centers of strong Christian movements during the early Christian centuries, with remnants surviving even today. In fact, Ethiopia is still politically a Christian nation. Also, it is probable that there have been several changes in their culture and/or ethnic structure during the 40 or so centuries of their existence, so that in effect there have really been significantly distinct nations in these countries from time to time. At present, Syria and Egypt, as well as many others in Africa and Asia, have become mainly Muslim nations, including practically all the nations surrounding Israel.

The numerous Muslim nations largely developed by conquest beginning in Arabia and spreading into Africa and central Asia, following the career of Mohammed and the rapid later inscripturation of his "revelations" in the Koran. Not all these nations are Arab nations, of course, though Mohammed was an Arab (claiming descent from Ishmael) and the Koran is written in Arabic. Arabia, however, is a very large peninsula, and the Bible indicates there were numerous kingdoms in Arabia. Several of the descendants of Shem (e.g., the sons of Joktan — Gen. 10:26–29), as well as the sons of Ishmael (Gen. 25:13–18) and of Abraham by Keturah (Gen. 25:1–4), seem to have founded city-states in Arabia. One of the sons of Keturah was ancestor of the Midianites, who seem to have merged with Ishmaelites (Gen. 37:25, 28) by the time of Jacob.

The phenomenon of the rapid spread of Islam and its continued dominance even today of many nations (from Algeria to Indonesia and from Sudan to Uzbekistan, all following the Koran) requires some kind of explanation. These nations are today considered somewhat backward technologically, but many of them did make many real contributions to science and technology during the Middle Ages. Furthermore, Islam is strongly monotheistic and does give a sort of enigmatic recognition to the Bible and to Christ. However, their time is certainly coming for judgment, since they are bitter enemies of Israel, and are bent on its destruction.

Two Bible chapters (Ps. 83 and Ezek. 38) seem to deal with God's future judgment on these Muslim nations. Psalm 83 deals with a confederation seeking to destroy Israel in the last days. The confederation consists of *"Edom and the Ishmaelites; of Moab and the Hagarenes; Gebal, and Ammon, and Amalek: the Philistines with the inhabitants of Tyre, Assur also . . ."* (Ps. 83:6–7). The nations currently surrounding and opposing Israel are composed of descendants of these ancient nations, after millennia of mergers and migrations. Similarly, Ezekiel 38 can be understood to speak of an organized latter-day attack on Israel by the Muslim nations of the old Soviet Union, plus Iran, Ethiopia, Libya, and others now surrounding Israel at greater distances than those mentioned in Psalm 83. In both chapters, the assurance is given of future supernatural deliverance by God and catastrophic defeat of all Israel's enemies.

It obviously is not feasible here to discuss each of the 200 or more present-day nations, not to mention all those of the past that have been superseded by still others. But if this were done, examining each nation in light of its attitude toward the true God, His moral law, and His chosen nation Israel, as well as its contribution to accomplishing God's primeval dominion mandate, these criteria would undoubtedly suggest the spiritual reasons for that nation's rise and fall in light of Acts 17:26, where we are told that God *"hath determined the times before appointed and the bounds of their habitation."* The next verse (Acts 17:27) says that their intended purpose (intended by God, that is) was *"that they might seek the Lord,"* as well as to continue under His dominion mandate, which has never been withdrawn.

As we shall discuss later, God has issued a second worldwide, age-long mandate, but this one only to believing men and women who are committed to the true God, not only as Creator but also, through Christ, as Redeeming Savior. This mandate has been called the Great Commission and involves evangelizing the unbelieving peoples of the world, seeking to win them to faith in the true God and Savior. The faithfulness of the believers in that nation to *this* mandate (in addition to the first) is surely another criterion on which God evaluates the nation and determines its appointed time.

Before ending this discussion of the origin and demise of each nation, we need to consider briefly the United States of America — often called simply America. Its origin involved the conquest of those nations previously inhabiting the land, the so-called Indian nations, and this has become in recent years the subject of severe criticism by many liberals in America, as well as all over the world.

However, it should be remembered that the Indian nations were frequently fighting other tribes and replacing others before them, too. They had accomplished very little in terms of the dominion mandate and had all rejected the true God in favor of various false gods. Their moral standards were low; even the culturally most advanced among them, such as the Aztec nation, practiced human sacrifice. It is not all that surprising that God allowed them to be replaced. America's founding, of course, was in large measure for the very purpose of building a nation under God. And God has signally blessed America, arguably more than any other nation in history.

But will America's time come to an end, also? We cannot predict the future, and there is no doubt that America's level of belief in Christianity and in practical biblical morality has dropped precipitously in modern times.

On the other hand, America's contribution to the dominion mandate has probably been greater than any nation before us, and our level of belief in the true God of creation is surely still greater than almost any other nation in the present world. Furthermore, America's contribution under the Great Commission is probably greater than any other modern nation, as well as its support of God's chosen nation Israel.

For these reasons, we can hope that America will continue indefinitely as an independent nation. But it is of great concern that her support of Israel, her leadership in world science and technology, her standards of morality, and even her commitment to the God of the Bible are all showing a serious tendency to decline. The modern creationism revival which has centered in America is a good sign, but prayer for the nation is surely needed in these critical days.

CHAPTER VI

THE CHOSEN NATION

For over 16 centuries, there were apparently no governments and *no nations* as such in the world, and this arrangement failed. God finally sent the world-destroying Deluge to cleanse the globe of its totally wicked inhabitants, so that He could, as it were, start over. The no-nations system, possibly with Noah as the head of all government, was allowed to continue for one more century, but then one of Noah's great grandsons, Nimrod, managed somehow to gain control and turn it all into a dictatorship with him as its head. This was almost as bad as having no nations or governments at all, at least in terms of opposition by the world to its Creator. God therefore forced the issue of forming many nations through the confusion of tongues at Babel.

For the next century or so, God dealt with a world of *many nations*. From no nations to one nation to many nations (proliferating gradually into many more, initially 70 of them, currently about 200) — that was what He had to deal with. But all of them failed, with Romans 1:20–28 describing the terrible apostasy of those first post-Babel nations. This led finally to God's preparation of one very special nation which He could use to bring His message and plan of redemption to the world.

The New Nation

That nation was Israel. However, it was not a nation to begin with, but only one man, Abraham, son of Terah and descendant of Shem.

At that time, Terah and his family, including Abram (Abraham's original name) were living in a large coastal city of the first Babylonians, or Chaldeans, known as Ur of the Chaldees. Terah had apparently been given custody of the ancient writings from Adam, Noah, and Shem, and had continued the inspired chronicle in what he called "the generations of Terah," amounting essentially only to the genealogical record from Shem to Abram (Gen. 11:11–27).

But then, somehow, according to Joshua 24:2, Terah began to allow the pagans among whom he was living to compromise his own faith so that he began to worship other "gods" in addition to the true God, Jehovah, and God had to give him up as well. Terah's son Abram was still a faithful believer, however, so God told him to leave his father and establish a new nation devoted only to the one true God.

> *Get thee out of thy country, and from thy kindred, and from thy father's house, unto a land that I will shew thee; And I will make of thee a great nation, and I will bless thee, and make thy name great; and thou shalt be a blessing: And I will bless them that bless thee, and curse him that curseth thee: and in thee shall all families of the earth be blessed* (Gen. 12:1–3).

The land to which the Lord directed Abram was already settled by descendants of Canaan, but they (like all the others) had departed far from God. Specifically, the boundaries of the land promised to Abram were delineated to him by God as follows:

> *Unto thy seed have I given this land, from the river of Egypt unto the great river, the river Euphrates* (Gen. 15:18).

The "river of Egypt" probably meant the Nile, although this is not certain. The *"river Euphrates"* is a long river, extending from Mount Ararat in northeastern Turkey down to the Persian Gulf. The promised boundaries seem to extend up through all the lands of Canaan and Syria to the northern reaches of the Euphrates. Its ultimate fulfillment will apparently be attained only in the coming millennium following Christ's return. More immediately included were the lands of the various Canaanite tribes, especially the Amorites, but even these were not immediately given to Abraham.

As a matter of fact, the only property ever owned by Abraham personally in the promised land was a cave he purchased from a Hittite in which he could bury his wife Sarah over 60 years later (Gen. 23). As the writer of Hebrews commented:

> By faith Abraham, when he was called to go out into a place which he should after receive for an inheritance, obeyed; and he went out, not knowing whither he went. By faith he sojourned in the land of promise, as in a strange country. . . . For he looked for a city which hath foundations, whose builder and maker is God (Heb. 11:8–10).

God's promise to Abraham was firmly renewed to Isaac and especially to Jacob, whose name was eventually changed by God to Israel, meaning "prevailing prince with God." It was Jacob (or Israel) whose 12 sons became the patriarchs of the 12 tribes of Israel.

However, their years of multiplication to the point of being a viable nation had to take place outside of the promised land, as slaves in Egypt. God had told Abraham:

> Know of a surety that thy seed shall be a stranger in a land that is not theirs, and shall serve them; and they shall afflict them four hundred years . . . for the iniquity of the Amorites is not yet full (Gen. 15:13–16).

As noted before, the Canaanite nations still were in their probational *"time appointed,"* when God first called Abram. But when the time finally came, the Children of Israel had grown to a population of over two million and were about ready to become a nation. First, however, there was a time of testing in the desert.

The Law

At this point in the preparation of Israel to be God's chosen nation, God raised up Moses. Providentially preserved while a babe, Moses had actually been raised up as a prince of Egypt, having been adopted — even though born of Hebrew parents — by the daughter of the reigning pharaoh, who had recently decreed that Hebrew baby boys all be killed, in order to prevent further growth of the Hebrew population.

As Moses grew, he became prominent as a leader in Pharaoh's military forces, at least according to traditions preserved in the writings of the Jewish historian Josephus, and could possibly have been in line even to become a future king of Egypt. God had a very different calling for him, however, and he became the leader of the Israelites instead, leading them in a remarkable exodus from Egypt and then a journey to God's land as promised to his ancestor Abraham long before.

During their 40-year wandering sojourn in the dreadful desert between Egypt and Canaan, they were actually being trained by Moses to be a strong and cohesive people, both militarily and spiritually. Those members of the 12 tribal units who were either rebellious or skeptical died off during that period, as the people were being miraculously fed and protected continuously by the Lord. Finally, as they were ready to enter and conquer the Promised Land, Moses turned the leadership over to Joshua and died without ever reaching it himself.

Nevertheless, he had made a uniquely vital contribution to the fulfillment of God's plan — not only for Israel, but also, indirectly, for all the nations of the world. He was not only an incomparable leader, but also a great writer and historian, writing the first five books of the Bible, the Pentateuch, while camping there in the *"waste howling wilderness"* (Deut. 32:10) of the Sinai desert.

Those five books — Genesis, Exodus, Leviticus, Numbers, Deuteronomy — are the foundational books of the Bible. Moses took the transmitted writings of the earlier patriarchs (Adam, Noah, Shem, Isaac, Jacob, and Joseph in particular), which had somehow been preserved by those great men through all the earlier ages, organizing and editing them into the Book of Genesis. The other four books of the were written by Moses himself, with the probable exception of the last chapter of Deuteronomy, describing Moses' death, most likely recorded by Joshua. It is very likely that the Book of Job, probably written by Job at least as early as the time of Abraham, had also been obtained by Moses and incorporated by him into what would eventually become the canonical books of the Old Testament. All of this was done, of course, in some inscrutable way, by the inspiration of the Holy Spirit, so that these writings of fallible human beings actually became part of the infallible, inerrant, written Word of God.

Other than these vital histories, the most important aspect of Moses' writings was the codification of the divine laws for the nation of Israel being formed there in the desert. As noted earlier, there had been legal codes before that of Moses — the code of Hammurabi in Babylon, the Hittite code, the Ebla code, and probably others, devised by and for various nations.

In fact, there had even been an earlier divine code of some sort, mentioned as having been observed by both Abraham and Job (note Gen. 26:5; Job 23:12). This has now been superseded by the Mosaic code, of course, whatever may have been its nature, but it is likely that Moses' laws, as well as those of these other ancient nations, reflect to some degree that earlier codification of God's commandments, especially in the ordinances related to civic matters.

The Mosaic law code obviously was structured by God specifically to apply to Israel, His elect nation. Its provisions are instructive and valuable as guides for any nation, but there are many portions specifically designed for the people of Israel — for example, the priesthood, the sacrifices, the feasts, the tabernacle worship, etc., as well as the heavy penalties for lawbreakers.

The essential core of the Mosaic Law, of course, consists of God's Ten Commandments (Exod. 20:1–17, repeated in Deut. 5:6–22). These are so familiar that they need not be quoted in full here. The essence of each is as follows:

1. Worship no "god" but the true God, the Creator of all things.
2. Make no likeness of anything or anyone for worship purposes.
3. Do not invoke God's name in either profanity or triviality.
4. Keep the weekly day of rest and worship.
5. Honor your parents.
6. Do not murder anyone.
7. Do not commit adultery (any sexual commerce except with one's spouse).
8. Do not steal anything.
9. Do not lie, particularly about a person.
10. Do not covet anything belonging to someone else.

These are all basic aspects of human behavior which are vital for any nation, even though specially directed toward Israel. The first four obviously focus on man's relation to God, the rest on man's relation to other men, the most important of all ten being the very first commandment.

While these commandments are valid universally, their importance is emphasized by the fact that *in Israel,* a flagrant violation of most of them was punishable by death — with the violator to be *"cut off from his people."* The phrase *"cut off from his people,"* occurs at least 20 times just in the books of Moses. Depending on context, "cut off" can mean either "execute" or "excommunicate." Even the latter punishment would amount to "consign to hell" and might well eventually also lead to physical death. In any case, the specified penalty was very drastic.

Just to give a few examples, the penalty for blasphemy (breaking any of the first three commandments), was clearly lethal.

> *He that sacrificeth unto any god, save unto the* LORD *only, he shall be utterly destroyed* (Exod. 22:20).

> *And he that blasphemeth the name of the* LORD, *he shall surely be put to death* (Lev. 24:16).

Breaking the Sabbath, the fourth commandment, was also a capital crime.

> *Whosoever doeth any work in the sabbath day, he shall surely be put to death* (Exod. 31:15).

And what about dishonoring one's parents?

> *He that smiteth his father, or his mother, shall be surely put to death. . . . And he that curseth his father, or his mother, shall surely be put to death* (Exod. 21:15–17).

Both murder and adultery were also punishable by death.

> *He that smiteth a man, so that he die, shall be surely put to death* (Exod. 21:12).

> *The man that committeth adultery with another man's wife . . . the adulterer and the adulteress shall surely be put to death* (Lev. 20:10).

Note also that such abnormal sexual practices, as incest, homosexuality, and bestiality were also capital crimes (e.g., Lev. 20:11–16). The crime of murder, of course, had been prescribed as punishable by death ever since the days of Noah (Gen. 9:6). A number of other actions, not specifically named in the Ten Commandments, were also listed as warranting execution — practicing witchcraft or sorcery or in any way seeking to communicate with spirits, for example. And there were others.

The people of Israel had been chosen as God's elect nation, and God demanded holiness from them, while also promising great blessings for obedience to His laws, both individually and nationally.

> *For thou art an holy people unto the LORD thy God, and the LORD hath chosen thee to be a peculiar people unto himself, above all the nations that are upon the earth* (Deut. 14:2).

> *The LORD shall open unto thee his good treasure, the heaven to give the rain unto thy land in his season, and to bless all the work of thine hand . . . if that thou hearken unto the commandments of the LORD thy God, which I command thee this day, to observe and to do them* (Deut. 28:12–13).

In addition to the Ten Commandments, there were numerous other ordinances and regulations, which were included in these Mosaic laws, all of which were intended to be obeyed by this special nation. The various sacrificial offerings, supervised by the official priesthood, were also a part of the system by which the people could obtain cleansing and forgiveness.

The Mosaic legal code was not intended for the nations in general, but only for Israel. Nevertheless, it reflected the mind of God, in particular His hatred of sin, and also His love for the men and women He had created, and in this sense, it *would be* valuable for all nations to understand and apply when feasible. In fact, He specifically described it as the best of all human governmental systems on earth. Note the following divine evaluation:

> *For what nation is there so great, who hath God so nigh unto them, as the LORD our God is in all things that we call upon him for? And what nation is there so great, that hath statutes and*

judgments so righteous as all this law, which I set before you this day?" (Deut. 4:7–8).

Many forms of government have been employed by different tribes and nations throughout history, but the theocracy described by God through Moses would — in God's own judgment — have been the best if it had ever been truly implemented. Many today recoil at the strictness and severity of God's laws as set forth in the Mosaic writings. Modern attempts to impose them in part, as in the period of Puritan rule in England and New England, have largely failed for various reasons related to the rebelliousness of the human heart. If it had ever been *truly* implemented, in spirit as well as practice, it would certainly have assured national righteousness, justice, and happiness as no other system has ever done. Both the fear of punishment for lawbreaking and the great blessings promised to those who loved and obeyed God's laws would have been the greatest of incentives to holiness.

At the time, the Israelites did not think the laws were unreasonable or impracticable. According to the record:

> *Moses came and told the people all the words of the LORD, and all the judgments: and all the people answered with one voice, and said, All the words which the LORD hath said we will do* (Exod. 24:3).

Many years later, and even after the Children of Israel had gone through the repeated periods of rebellion, apostasy, and divine punishment during the period of the judges, King David could still testify enthusiastically that:

> *The law of the LORD is perfect, converting* [same word as "restoring"] *the soul. . . . The statutes of the LORD are right, rejoicing the heart: the commandment of the LORD is pure, enlightening the eyes. . . . the judgments of the LORD are true and righteous altogether. . . . Moreover by them is thy servant warned: and in keeping of them there is great reward* (Ps. 19:7–11).

Consider also the remarkable testimony of the unknown Israelite who wrote the longest chapter in the Bible, the 119th Psalm, practically every verse of which is a worshipful comment on God's written Word

— which at that time consisted mainly of these writings of Moses, especially the law. Note just a few of his comments, chosen essentially at random.

I will delight myself in thy statutes (v. 16).

Behold, I have longed after thy precepts (v. 40).

And I will delight myself in thy commandments, which I have loved (v. 47).

O how love I thy law! it is my meditation all the day (v. 97).

I rejoice at thy word (v. 162).

Great peace have they which love thy law (v. 165).

This hardly sounds like God's law was too harsh! Except during those times of apostasy, the people of God loved it and obeyed it, so that there were few occasions on which its rigorous penalties had to be enforced — so few that when one did take place, it was actually included in the divine record (e.g., the stoning of a man for gathering sticks on the Sabbath — see Num. 15:32–36). Certainly most of the recorded instances of actual capital punishment had to do with blasphemy and idolatry, and these were necessary to maintain the distinctive character of the Children of Israel as the elect nation of the true God.

The Law in an Age of Grace

Although this chapter is primarily concerned with Israel and the Mosaic laws, the question frequently arises as to whether Christian nations are supposed to keep these laws now that *"Christ has redeemed us from the curse of the law"* (Gal. 3:13). Many have argued that the law has been completely superseded by grace and we have been set free from the law and its demands.

It is obvious that we cannot be saved by keeping the law. *"For by the works of the law shall no flesh be justified"* (Gal. 2:16), one main reason being that no person (except the Lord Jesus) ever has kept or ever could keep all the law perfectly. *"For whosoever shall keep the whole law, and yet offend in one point, he is guilty of all"* (James 2:10).

Nevertheless, the law does reveal the holiness of God, especially the Ten Commandments, so the true Christian (like the Psalmist) will love God's law and seek to honor it to the best of his ability — not out of fear of punishment for failure but out of love and gratitude for his forgiveness and salvation. He may not be under the law of Moses, but he *is* under *"the law of Christ"* (Gal. 6:2).

And what is that? Jesus said, *"A new commandment I give unto you, That ye love one another; as I have loved you, that ye also love one another"* (John 13:34). Jesus also gave many other specific commands as to how this love should be expressed, and said, *"If ye love me, keep my commandments"* (John 14:15).

The ceremonial aspects of the Mosaic laws, of course, were done away in Christ. The animal sacrifices, the officiating priesthood, all such ritualistic ceremonies, meaningful as they were at the time, are no more needed, *"for by one offering [Christ] hath perfected for ever them that are sanctified"* (Heb. 10:14).

Nevertheless, as far as the Ten Commandments are concerned at least, it is significant that every one of them has been reiterated in the New Testament, as expressing God's will for Christian believers — not as conditions of salvation but as appropriate characteristics of a genuine Christian life. Note just briefly some typical New Testament Scriptures relating to each of the Ten Commandments in turn:

No. 1: *"Thou shalt love the Lord thy God with all thy heart, and with all thy soul, and with all thy mind, and with all thy strength: this is the first commandment"* (Mark 12:30).

No. 2: *"Neither be ye idolaters, as were some of them"* (1 Cor. 10:7).

No. 3: *"But I say unto you, Swear not at all"* (Matt. 5:34).

No. 4: *"There remaineth therefore a rest [literally a 'Sabbath rest'] to the people of God"* (Heb. 4:9).

No. 5: *"Honour thy father and mother; which is the first commandment with promise"* (Eph. 6:2).

No. 6: *"Let none of you suffer as a murderer"* (1 Pet. 4:15).

No. 7: *"Whoremongers and adulterers God will judge"* (Heb. 13:4).

No. 8: *"Let him that stole steal no more"* (Eph. 4:28).

No. 9: *"Lie not one to another"* (Col. 3:9).

No. 10: *"No . . . covetous man . . . hath any inheritance in the kingdom of Christ and of God"* (Eph. 5:5).

There are numerous other New Testament references to the same effect. As Paul said, *"Wherefore the law is holy, and the commandment holy, and just, and good. . . . For I delight in the law of God after the inward man"* (Rom. 7:12–22). We ought, therefore, as Christians, to love and obey God's laws. In fact, we should go far beyond mere outward obedience to the letter of the law. Our Lord Jesus pointed out that anger and slander could be equivalent to murder, and lust to adultery (Matt. 5:21, 22, 27, 28). Neither Paul nor anyone else can be saved by keeping the law, but we should honor and obey the law as best we can *because* we are saved, by grace through faith in God's gift of love in Christ on the cross.

Why God Chose an Elect Nation

Why was Israel selected as God's chosen nation? It was not for any obvious external reasons.

> *The LORD did not set his love upon you, nor choose you, because ye were more in number than any people; for ye were the fewest of all people: But because the LORD loved you, and because he would keep the oath which he had sworn unto your fathers, hath the LORD brought you out with a mighty hand, and redeemed you out of the house of bondmen, from the hand of Pharaoh king of Egypt* (Deut. 7:7–8).

And just why did the Lord love Israel like this and do all this? It was not because of anything at all about the Israelites themselves, but

> *. . . because he loved thy fathers, therefore he chose their seed after them, and brought thee out in his sight with his mighty power out of Egypt* (Deut. 4:37).

Because of the great faith and character of Abraham, Isaac, and Jacob, God made an unconditional promise to them and their descendants — *that* was why He chose Israel!

> *By faith he [Abraham] sojourned in the land of promise, as in a strange country, dwelling in tabernacles [tents] with Isaac and Jacob, the heirs with him of the same promise* (Heb. 11:9).

> *He [Abraham] . . . was strong in faith, giving glory to God; And being fully persuaded that, what he had promised, he was able also to perform* (Rom. 4:20–21).

But why did He need to choose a special nation at all? In addition to the obvious reason that all the existing nations had become apostate at Babel, there were two other main reasons why He had to choose and prepare a special nation.

First of all, He had promised from the very beginning that the *"seed of the woman"* would eventually come to redeem the lost world from sin and death (Gen. 3:15). That "seed" would have to be a man, but one not born with a sin-nature like all other men, and that meant that God himself would have to become a man. He would have to be virgin-born in some human family, and therefore in some human nation. Consequently, a nation would have to be prepared to receive Him as a babe and nurture Him to adulthood.

Secondly, all nations would need to know about His coming and His provision for man's redemption. There would have to be a written revelation, or series of revelations, both before His coming to prepare the nation for it, and after His coming, to acquaint its people with its accomplishment and what is to follow.

Those revelations would have to be given in human language, which means the language of some particular human nation, though they could, and should, then be translated into the languages of other nations. Initially, of course, some nation must be designated to receive these revelations, and that would obviously be the same elect nation.

So there would have to be a nation selected to receive both God's Word and God's Son. These were surely two main reasons why God had to choose a nation, and the main reason why Israel was chosen was because of the faith of its fathers.

The apostle Paul confirmed the importance of these reasons, and then the tragic rejection by Israel of their significance.

> *What advantage then hath the Jew? . . . Much every way: chiefly, because that unto them were committed the oracles of God* (Rom. 3:1–2).

> *For I could wish that myself were accursed from Christ for my brethren, my kinsmen according to the flesh: Who are Israelites; to whom pertaineth the adoption, and the glory, and the covenants, and the giving of the law, and the service of God, and the promises; Whose are the fathers, and of whom as concerning the flesh Christ came, who is over all, God blessed for ever. Amen* (Rom. 9:3–5).

What a tragedy it was — for Israel, that is — for the Jews to reject the main purpose of the Mosaic law in which they took such great pride (that purpose being to serve as — *"our schoolmaster to bring us unto Christ, that we might be justified by faith"* Gal. 3:24) when they rejected Christ (that is, their promised Messiah) when He finally came. For Christ was not just the promised *"seed of the woman,"* but the woman in whose womb that holy seed had been sown by God himself was herself of *"the seed of Abraham"* and *"the seed of David"* (Heb. 2:16; Rom. 1:3).

Furthermore, God had used Israelites exclusively as the prophets who would receive and inscripturate His series of revelations. Not only Moses, David, Isaiah, and all the authors of the Old Testament Scriptures, but also the writers of the New Testament (with some uncertainty about Luke) were Jews.

And yet most of the Jews of Jesus' day, as well as those of every generation since, have continued to reject Him, both as their promised Messiah and also as God's promised Redeemer. They had served their purpose in bringing both the Scriptures and the Savior into the world through their nation, so a number of professedly Christian denominations and organizations believe that God has finished with them, now that they have repudiated Christ.

However, God's original promise to Abraham was unconditional. *"I say then, Hath God cast away his people? God forbid"* (Rom. 11:1). As a matter of fact, Israel was temporarily set aside as a nation, so that

God could deal with the Gentiles for a period of time. *"For . . . blindness in part is happened to Israel, until the fulness of the Gentiles be come in. And so all Israel shall be saved: as it is written, There shall come out of Sion the Deliverer, and shall turn away ungodliness from Jacob: For this is my covenant until then, when I shall take away their sins"* (Rom. 11:25–27).

CHAPTER VII

THE TIMES OF THE GENTILES

Although God has not abandoned Israel as His chosen nation, many centuries have come and gone while they have been under His severe hand of chastening, just as their prophets had predicted and warned.

> *For the children of Israel shall abide many days without a king, and without a prince, and without a sacrifice, and without an image, and without an ephod, and without teraphim* (Hos. 3:4).

It has indeed been *"many days"* (over 2,500 years) since Nebuchadnezzar destroyed Jerusalem and Solomon's beautiful temple. He then deposed King Zedekiah, slaying Zedekiah's sons just before his captors put out his own eyes (2 Kings 25:7). The use of images and teraphim and other idolatrous practices was apparently abandoned by the Israelites while they were in captivity in Babylon. Although they were later able to reestablish their sacrificial system after their return from captivity, even that was stopped when the Romans destroyed their later temple (built by King Herod) and dispersed the entire nation throughout the Roman world.

Even though many later returned to Israel, and even though the United Nations agreed to give them back their homeland, establishing a new nation of Israel in 1948, they are still without a king and without a sacrifice and an officiating priesthood (ephod, etc.). The political structure of the modern nation of Israel is almost entirely secular, with only a nominal commitment to their unique position and responsibilities as God's chosen nation.

During the days of the prophets, between the reigns of Solomon and Zedekiah, they had been repeatedly warned of God's coming judgment and their eventual banishment because of their frequent lapses into idolatry and resulting moral degeneration. Even before that, Moses had prophesied to that effect.

> The LORD shall scatter thee among all people, from the one end of the earth even unto the other . . . And among these nations shalt thou find no ease, neither shall the sole of thy foot have rest: but the LORD shall give thee there a trembling heart, and failing of eyes, and sorrow of mind: And thy life shall hang in doubt before thee: and thou shalt fear day and night, and shalt have none assurance of thy life (Deut. 28:64–66).

There were many other prophecies to the same effect.

At the same time, God also promised through Moses and the prophets that He would never abandon them completely.

> And yet for all that, when they be in the land of their enemies, I will not cast them away . . . to break my covenant with them: for I am the LORD their God (Lev. 26:44).

> Afterward shall the children of Israel return, and seek the LORD their God . . . in the latter days (Hos. 3:5).

As a matter of fact, the remarkable preservation of the Israelites as a distinct people through over two millennia of subjugation and worldwide dispersion is in itself a remarkable testimony to the divine origin of the Bible and to the unique nature of Israel among all the other nations. No other nation has been without a country of their own for such a long time and yet survived as a distinct national entity.

> Lo, the people shall dwell alone, and shall not be reckoned among the nations (Num. 23:9).

The Promised Messiah

Even during the dark days of apostasy, as well as in the days of God's blessing, the Children of Israel were often being reminded that a

Savior was coming. He was called the Messiah, meaning the "Anointed One." The very first such prophecy, of course, was the so-called "protevangelium," or "first gospel" (Gen. 3:15), in which God promised that "the woman's seed" would eventually crush the head of the serpent and all his evil designs.

As the years rolled by, the Messianic prophecies became more and more specific. Future spiritual "rest" would come through Noah's family (Gen. 5:29), then "blessing" through the seed of Abraham, Isaac, and Jacob (Gen. 12:3; 26:24; 28:14).

Of the 12 "Children of Israel" — that is, of Jacob — it was prophesied that *"the scepter"* would be with the tribe of Judah until the coming of *"Shiloh"* (Gen. 49:10), evidently a reference to the Messiah. And of all the descendants of Judah, David was chosen as king, with the promise that one of his descendants would occupy his throne forever (2 Sam. 7:16).

Many of the psalms in the Book of Psalms, especially those written by David, are Messianic psalms (e.g., Ps. 2, 8, 16, 22, 40, 68, 72, 102, 110). The prophets after David and Solomon predicted many of the aspects of Messiah's person and work. Isaiah, for example, predicted that Messiah would enter the human family through a virgin birth (Isa. 7:14), but that He would simultaneously continue to be *"the mighty God"* (Isa. 9:6). Micah revealed that He would be born in Bethlehem, but also revealed that His *"goings forth have been from of old, from everlasting"* (Mic. 5:2). Daniel even predicted the time of His coming (Dan. 9:25).

Many of the prophets told that He would indeed occupy the throne of David and that, as king over the nation of Israel, He would also be king over all the other nations as well. For example, the Psalmist (possibly David himself, possibly Solomon, or one of the later writers), said:

> *He shall have dominion also from sea to sea, and from the river unto the ends of the earth . . . Yea, all kings shall fall down before him: all nations shall serve him. . . . His name shall endure for ever; his name shall be continued as long as the sun: and men shall be blessed in him: all nations shall call him blessed. . . . And blessed be his glorious name for ever: and let the whole earth be filled with his glory; Amen, and amen (Ps. 72:8–19).*

The post-exilic prophet Zechariah summarized all such prophecies in the last chapter of his own prophecy, when he said:

> And the LORD shall be king over all the earth: in that day shall there be one LORD, and his name one (Zech. 14:9).

Yet, with all these glorious pictures of God's future blessing on His nation Israel through Messiah, a very different note was sounded through certain other key prophecies. Messiah would be rejected by His people, endure terrible suffering, and finally be slain. For example, the same prophet Isaiah, who often wrote so glowingly of Messiah's future worldwide reign in righteousness (Isa. 2, 11, 65, etc.) also wrote concerning His suffering and death.

> He hath no form nor comeliness; and when we shall see him, there is no beauty that we should desire him. He is despised and rejected of men; a man of sorrows, and acquainted with grief; and we hid as it were our faces from him; he was despised, and we esteemed him not (Isa. 53:2–3).

And Zechariah prophesied that Messiah would be *"pierced"* and *"wounded in the house of my friends"* (Zech. 12:10; 13:6) after being sold to His executioner for *"thirty pieces of silver"* (Zech. 11:12), the price of a slave.

How could such treatment be given to the One who had come to Israel to be their Redeemer, and how could such discrepant prophecies be reconciled? Isaiah gives the answer in that most wonderful Old Testament exposition of the New Testament gospel of salvation.

> But he was wounded for our transgressions, he was bruised for our iniquities: the chastisement of our peace was upon him; and with his stripes we are healed. . . . for he was cut off out of the land of the living: for the transgression of my people was he stricken (Isa. 53:5–8).

The Messiah (that is, Christ, for "Christ" is the Greek equivalent of the Hebrew word "Messiah") would indeed die as a substitute for the people of Israel, who fully deserved to be put to death for their many sins — the most grievous being their rejection of their long-awaited Messiah when He finally came.

That would, however, by no means be the end of God's relation with His chosen nation.

> *When thou shalt make his soul an offering for sin, he shall see his seed, he shall prolong his days* (Isa. 53:10).

That is, after His sacrificial death, He would be raised from the dead, and *"prolong his days."* In fact, He would be *"alive for evermore"* (Rev. 1:18), able indeed now to fulfill all His promises concerning Israel's glorious future.

There were a number of other prophecies of Messiah's death and resurrection, most notably in David's graphic prophetic description of His future crucifixion as given in Psalm 22. After describing the suffering in amazing detail, the Psalmist goes on to say that, afterwards, *"All the ends of the world shall remember and turn unto the LORD: and all the kindreds of the nations shall worship before thee. For the kingdom is the LORD's: and he is the governor among the nations"* (Ps. 22:27–28).

Therefore, His death and resurrection would apply not just for Israel, but for all nations. He would, indeed, die for the sins of His people Israel, but for the sins of Gentiles as well, for they also had been created in His image and were the objects of His eternal purposes.

Jews and the Gentiles

All these many prophecies, both concerning the Messiah and the nation Israel itself, are interspersed throughout the Old Testament, which in essence is simply a history of Israel down to the Babylonian exile and return. The record deals only peripherally with the Gentile nations, even then focusing almost altogether on only their contacts with Israel.

To begin with, Abraham was called out of the Chaldean nation specifically to form a new nation, which God would use to bring the Scriptures and the promised Savior (that is, the written Word and the Living Word) into the world. Then, during his eventful lifetime, Abraham had significant contacts with many other nations — Egypt, Philistia, Sumeria, Elam, etc. — as well as the Canaanites in the land that God had promised to his seed. His first son, Ishmael, founded another nation (which later proliferated into several more nations), and the sons of his nephew Lot founded the nations of Moab and Ammon. His second (and promised) son Isaac married a woman (actually a relative) of Abraham's former home in Syria. One of Isaac's own sons in turn became the founder of the nation of Edom. Furthermore, Abraham's later sons by his second wife, Keturah, established their own clans, of which the Midianite nation became the most prominent. Many of these various nation-states have, over the years, gradually merged to become what are known today as the Arab nations. These mostly tend to claim descent from Ishmael and, like their distant progenitor, have frequently (especially today!) been in conflict with the children of Jacob.

After spending a long time as slaves in Egypt, Moses and Joshua led the Children of Israel into the promised land of Canaan. In addition, Moses somehow had married a woman from the nation of Ethiopia, as well as a woman of Midian.

Many of the nations listed in the Table of Nations (Gen. 10) are referred to from time to time in the Old Testament as having at least incidental contact with Israel. Note, for example, mentions of Gomer, Meshech, Tubal, Magog, Togarma, Sheba, Dedan, and Tarshish in Ezekiel 38 (verses 2, 3, 6, and 13), all evidently still viable nations in Ezekiel's time during the Babylonian exile of Judah. Many other examples could be cited.

The point of this mention of many nations is that, although the Old Testament is mainly a record of God's dealings with Israel as His elect nation, both God and Israel were very much aware of the other nations of the ancient world. God had not forgotten them. As noted before, God had purposes for all of them, setting the bounds of their habitations and their appointed times (Acts 17:26) in accordance with those purposes. This becomes especially evident later in the Book of Daniel.

Before this, however, the nation Israel had enjoyed over 800 years of somewhat checkered existence as a nation among nations, reaching its greatest power and influence under Kings David and Solomon (by way of comparison, note that our own nation, the United States, has existed as an independent nation only some 230 years thus far, less than a third as long as Israel did). After Solomon, however, the nation divided. The southern kingdom consisted mainly of the tribes of Judah and Benjamin, although many of the Levites and Simeonites remained in Judah, as well as remnants of the others. It became known as the Kingdom of Judah, and its citizens as Jews. The northern kingdom consisted of the other ten tribes (with both Ephraim and Manasseh, the two sons of Joseph, considered as separate tribes).

Unhappily, the ten-tribe northern kingdom, which continued to be called Israel, had a series of ungodly apostates, beginning with Jeroboam I, as king, leading their kingdom deeper and deeper into idolatry. Perhaps the worst of these was Ahab, of whom it was said that he *"did evil in the sight of the LORD above all that were before him"* (1 Kings 16:30).

His wickedness was aggravated by his wife, Jezebel, whose very name has become a symbol of evil women in later ages. Jezebel was from Phoenicia, a great but idolatrous nation of the ancient world. The two of them made Baal the chief deity of Israel, and led almost the whole nation into apostasy and Baal worship (although God told the prophet Elijah that there were still *"seven thousand in Israel, all the knees which have not bowed unto Baal"* (1 Kings 19:18).

Elijah and his successor, Elisha, were courageous, devout, and miracle-working prophets in Israel during those days, but their preaching was only verbal, not written. Among the writing prophets, Hosea and Amos prophesied mainly concerning Israel, but their prophecies availed little, as Israel descended further into sin. Finally, God's patience was exhausted.

> The LORD testified against Israel, and against Judah, by all the prophets, and by all the seers, saying, Turn ye from your evil ways, and keep my commandments and my statutes, according to all the law which I commanded your fathers, and which I sent to you by my servants the prophets. Notwithstanding they would not hear, but hardened their necks, like to the neck of their fathers, that did not believe in the LORD their God. . . . Therefore, the LORD was very angry with Israel, and removed them out of his sight: there was none left but the tribe of Judah only (2 Kings 17:13–18).

He removed them all the way to Assyria by its king Shalmaneser. The southern kingdom of Judah was also threatened by the Assyrians, but the prayers of Judah's good king Hezekiah were answered, and Jerusalem was delivered, for a time at least.

Judah did, in fact, have several prophets (Isaiah, Jeremiah, etc.), as well as a number of good kings who tried to lead their nation back to God (Asa, Jehoshaphat, Joash, Jotham, Hezekiah, Josiah), but all these kings tended to compromise in one way or another, and finally could not overcome the influence of Judah's wicked kings (Ahaz, Manasseh, Amon, Jeconiah, etc.), causing God eventually to send Judah also into captivity. Judah did survive as an independent nation over 100 years longer than the northern kingdom of Israel, but eventually they too were captured by Nebuchadnezzar and sent into exile in Babylon (which, in the meantime, had conquered Assyria).

> *And the LORD God of their fathers sent to them by his messengers, rising up betimes, and sending; because he had compassion on his people, and on his dwelling place: But they mocked the messengers of God, and despised his words, and misused his prophets, until the wrath of the LORD arose against his people, till there was no remedy* (2 Chron. 36:15–16).

Thus both kingdoms, Judah and Israel, finally became so wicked and apostate that God allowed ungodly enemies (Babylonia and Assyria) to destroy their capitals (Jerusalem and Samaria, respectively) and carry the best of their people as slaves away from their promised land. The ten tribes of the northern kingdom never returned from Assyria as a nation, although many individuals no doubt eventually got back home. Judah, however, was finally allowed to return by the Persians, and did rebuild Jerusalem and the temple, though not to its former glory. Even that restoration was only temporary, however. When their Messiah finally appeared, they rejected and crucified Him, as the prophets had foreseen, and they were soon thereafter dispersed by their Roman rulers throughout the world, with their city and temple again destroyed.

The Rule of the Gentiles

Although the Jews retained a semblance of independence after their return from exile, especially under the leadership of the Macabees, they were never again completely free from outside jurisdiction. Thus, the period beginning with the Babylonian exile, and continuing ever since, could well be called the "times of the Gentiles."

The greatest empires before Babylon's rise had been Sumeria, Egypt, and Assyria. In fact, Sumeria could be considered the first Babylon, although the ethnicity of its citizens had changed. At this key moment in the history of Israel, with the dominant tribe of Judah no longer independent but deported to Babylon, God gave to the prophet Daniel, by way of Nebuchadnezzar, a remarkable foreview of all subsequent Gentile world history.

Daniel was a very talented and godly young man of the tribe of Judah, who had been taken, along with others, as captives to Babylon by King Nebuchadnezzar. By God's grace and His providential leading, Daniel became very prominent and influential in Babylon, serving for many years as advisor to King Nebuchadnezzar and (later) to King Darius of the Persians who had conquered Babylon in the meantime, then (still later) to King Cyrus of Persia.

King Nebuchadnezzar had had a disturbing dream about a great image, with a head of gold, breast and arms of silver, belly and thighs of brass, and legs of iron, with feet of a clay/iron mixture. The feet had then been shattered by a great stone somehow cut out of a mountain without hands. The whole image then collapsed into dust while the shattering stone became a great mountain which filled the whole earth.

Daniel alone, of all the wise men of Babylon, was not only able to recall to the king his troubling dream but also to tell him what it meant. God had indeed revealed to him that the world's future would devolve around four great kingdoms which would dominate world history. These are easily interpretable in retrospect as Babylonia, Medo-Persia, Greece, and Rome, in that chronological order, with the final phase (the strength of Rome mixed with the weakness of humanism) to be succeeded suddenly by a great kingdom established by God himself.

And surely that remarkable prophetic vision has been fulfilled in subsequent history. World events have indeed been dominated successively by these four empires. The last, that of Rome, lasted longer than any of the others (as represented by the legs of the image), and in fact still exists in the legal, linguistic, political, and militaristic structures of the many western Gentile nations that emerged from the old Roman empire, especially in Europe and America.

Rome was in power, of course, at the time Messiah, the Lord Jesus Christ, finally came into the world. He fulfilled all the old Messianic prophecies — His miraculous birth, life, teachings, etc., especially those dealing with His substitutionary death and wonderful victory over death — except those promising the ultimate defeat of Satan and His glorious reign over all the nations.

These latter had to be deferred because of His rejection by the Jewish nation and, indeed, by the Gentiles as well. Instead of joyfully acknowledging Him as their long-awaited Savior and King, the Jewish leaders were complicit with their Gentile rulers in His crucifixion.

Consequently, the Lord Jesus wept over His beloved city, Jerusalem, making yet another Messianic prediction:

> *O Jerusalem . . . Behold your house is left unto you desolate. For I say unto you, Ye shall not see me henceforth, till ye shall say, Blessed is he that cometh in the name of the Lord* (Matt. 23:37–39).

And just when would that be? Note also His other fateful words.

> *And when he was come near, he beheld the city, and wept over it, Saying, If thou hadst known, even thou, at least in this thy day, the things which belong unto thy peace! but now they are hid from thine eyes. For the days shall come upon thee, that thine enemies . . . shall lay thee even with the ground, and thy children within thee: and they shall not leave in thee one stone upon another, because thou knewest not the time of thy visitation* (Luke 19:41–44).

All of this terrible judgment took place just a few years later, in A.D. 70, when the Roman army under Titus completely destroyed the beautiful temple, tearing it down stone by stone. But as to when the Jews would finally accept Him as their Savior and King, He made yet another prophecy:

> *And they shall fall by the edge of the sword, and shall be led away captive into all nations: and Jerusalem shall be trodden down of the Gentiles, until the times of the Gentiles shall be fulfilled* (Luke 21:24).

For almost 2,000 years the Jews have indeed been wandering among all the nations of the world, grievously persecuted in many nations, yet continuing to reject Christ, although the orthodox among them continue to look for Messiah's coming to establish His worldwide kingdom centered at Jerusalem.

But that cannot happen until they acknowledge that Messiah has already come, and testify: Blessed is He that cometh in the name of the Lord. Then, the times of the Gentiles shall be fulfilled, *"And the LORD shall be king over all the earth: in that day shall there be one LORD, and his name one"* (Zech. 14:9).

That that day is probably very near seems indicated by the fact that Jerusalem once again is home and capital to the Jews. The nation of Israel was recognized by the United Nations (representing, supposedly, all the Gentile nations of the world) back in 1948, after the Zionist movement had enabled the return of many Jews to their former homeland — the land that by then had come to be called Palestine, largely a barren land occupied mainly by a number of small Arab villages along with a few nominally Christian churches and a handful of Jews.

Since 1948, the productivity of the land has been largely restored by the industry of the Zionist settlers, and Israel has become a thriving nation with millions of energetic and enthusiastic Jewish citizens, now known officially as Israelis.

It would seem that many of the prophecies concerning the return of the Jews have been fulfilled, but the tragedy is that, even though Jerusalem seems to have been recovered by the Jews (or Israelis) as their capital, they are largely secular Jews and have even rejected the Old Testament, let alone rejecting Jesus as their Messiah and Savior. Consequently, "the times of the Gentiles" have not yet been fulfilled.

In fact, the Palestinian Arabs are still bitterly opposed to Israel, determined to drive them out of what they now claim to be *their* homeland. Several wars have been fought, but the Israelis thus far have triumphed, and still control Jerusalem.

Except its most vital location, that is! The "temple mount," where their temple once stood, is occupied by a Muslim mosque and controlled by the Muslim Arabs of Palestine. *That* particular plot of ground *is* Jerusalem, as far as orthodox Jewry is concerned. They cannot yet rebuild their temple, and thus Jerusalem in a very real sense is not yet under Jewish control and *"the times of the Gentiles"* are not yet fulfilled. And certainly the Israelis have not yet said: *"Blessed be he* [that is, the Lord Jesus] *that cometh in the name of the Lord."* In fact, they bitterly oppose Christian missions in Israel and despise the growing number of individual Jews who are accepting Christ personally.

In the meantime, however, for two thousand years, the saving gospel of Christ has been preached among the Gentiles, and some in practically every nation of the world have acknowledged Him as Savior and Lord. As that great Jewish Christian, the apostle Paul, wrote to the Gentiles:

> *Through their fall salvation is come unto the Gentiles . . . Behold therefore the goodness and severity of God: on them which fell, severity: but toward thee, goodness . . . For as ye in times past have not believed God, yet now have obtained mercy through their unbelief . . . O the depth of the riches both of the wisdom and knowledge of God!* (Rom. 11:11–33).

CHAPTER VIII

THE NATIONS TODAY

As noted previously, God is now visiting *"the Gentiles, to take out of them a people for his name"* (Acts 15:14), thereby creating a new nation, the Church, composed of people from every human nation on earth who have trusted Christ for salvation and been *"born again."* That "nation" does not have a capital or a king here on earth, Vatican City and its pope notwithstanding.

"For our conversation is in heaven" (Phil. 3:20). The word translated *"conversation"* in this verse is the Greek *politeuma*, which actually means "citizenship." That is, while we may be citizens of the United States or some other nation here in this world, we are also citizens of the heavenly kingdom, which is none other than *"the everlasting kingdom of our Lord and Saviour Jesus Christ"* (2 Pet. 1:11).

This kingdom is actually called *"an holy nation"* (1 Peter 2:9), and while Christians are frequently exhorted to be good citizens of our particular nation here on earth *"for the Lord's sake"* (e.g., 1 Pet. 2:13–17), our primary allegiance is to God (Acts 5:29) and we are, in effect, *"ambassadors for Christ"* here on earth (2 Cor. 5:20). When we trusted Christ for our salvation, God *"translated us into the kingdom of his dear Son"* (Col. 1:13), so that is where our home really is, now and forever.

Thus, there are now three special "nations" in particular here on the earth — *"the Jews, the Gentiles, and the church of God"* (1 Cor. 10:32) — that is: the Jewish people as a whole, including the actual nation of Israel plus all the Jews still scattered around the world;

secondly, all the Gentile nations viewed as a group; and thirdly, the born-again Christians from every nation.

That does not imply, however, that the established earthly nations — England, Egypt, China, etc. — are no longer of interest to God as nations. Remember that God *"hath determined the times before appointed, and the bounds of their habitation"* in every case for the individual nations, having made *"all nations of men for to dwell on all the face of the earth"* (Acts 17:26).

Many nations of the past no longer exist as anything but small remnant populations, having failed in their God-given opportunities and passed their appointed times — nations such as the great Babylonian empire, the Aztec empire, the Mayans, the Incas, the Scythians, the Hittites, and many others. But there are now perhaps 200 viable nations as such functioning today, some of the greatest being the United States, the United Kingdom, Russia, China, Germany, India, Japan, and several others. These are all still under active observation by God in terms of their faithfulness in seeking Him and in accomplishing His primeval dominion mandate.

The Ongoing Dominion Mandate

Although most and probably all the world's present nations are no longer even aware of it, the fact remains that God's primeval dominion mandate has never been withdrawn, and thus is still in effect. As discussed in chapter II, it was given originally to Adam and Eve, then confirmed and expanded to Noah after the great flood. These two patriarchs are the "first fathers" (which is the very meaning of the word "patriarch") of every person and therefore every nation in the world, so the mandate has clearly been passed on to us.

It is, therefore, appropriate to raise the question as to how well the dominion mandate is being implemented by the present nations. The very first component in the mandate was the establishment of monogamous life-long marriage as the basis for producing the population needed to accomplish the other components of the mandate.

It is immediately obvious that the nations have failed miserably in this aspect. The nominally Christian nations of the west have given priority to monogamy in their legal codes, but divorce and "serial" polygamy have become very common, and now even cohabitation without marriage. In the United States (arguably the most nearly "Christian" of all nations), it is now generally acknowledged that half of all current marriages end in divorce. Adultery, fornication, and general immorality have proliferated alarmingly, and abortion of unwanted children is widespread.

Although various liberals have decried what they think is a "population explosion," the fact is that the birth rate has fallen to the extent that future populations in the nominally Christian nations will decline, rather than grow. This is even more true in Europe and other "developed" nations than in America. God said to *"fill"* the earth, but there are vast deserts and uninhabitable regions all over the world. The projected decline in the populations of technologically advanced and prosperous nations has even led some key scholars to predict the imminent "death of the west."

Furthermore, this alarming trend is exacerbated by the terrible plague of abortions and by the growing practice and promotion of homosexuality, along with the proliferation of AIDS and other sexually transmitted diseases that is accompanying it. God certainly is bound to be disappointed, to put it mildly, at this aspect of the way His dominion mandate is being carried out.

And it is not only in the advanced nations that this failure is obvious. The many Moslem nations of the world flagrantly disobey the mandate. The Koran allows each man to have four wives, as well as easy divorce. They do, of course, generate large populations, but these are hardly contributing much to the other components of the mandate (science, technology, education, etc.). China and India have contributed abundantly toward filling the earth with people, and so have the African nations. All seem envious of the western nations in terms of technology and prosperity, a situation which has led to great tensions and many local wars and revolutions.

As far as *"subduing the earth"* is concerned, many nations have made significant contributions in terms of science, technology, commerce, education, and cultural products, although it is bound to be more than coincidence that the most important such contributions have come from Europe and America. The writer's mother (born in 1899, died in 1983), used to boast how she had lived during such an amazing century, with transportation initially by horse and buggy, then automobile, airplane, and space ship. In a similar time period, communications have been delivered by pony express, stage coach, railroad, telegraph, telephone, air mail, and e-mail. Many writers have pointed out how these and other aspects of civilization changed very little for thousands of years, then in one century developed more than in all previous history. Students of Bible prophecy, in fact, have pointed out that all this is a sign of the soon coming of Christ, citing Daniel 12:4 in particular: *"But thou, O Daniel, shut up the words, and seal the book, even to the time of the end: many shall run to and fro, and knowledge shall be increased."*

In spite of all this advance in science and technology, however, mankind is still a long way from subduing the earth. Much of his great knowledge, of course, has been directed to useless or harmful ends — more sophisticated and deadly warfare, for example, or the development and popularization of deadly drugs, or the greater undermining of moral standards by sophisticated techniques in movies and television, or even just increased time for play and leisure or other unproductive activities. Yet we have not been able to control the weather or make the great deserts fertile and habitable or develop cures for numerous deadly diseases (cancer, Alzheimer's, muscular sclerosis, etc.).

Long ago, God described the patriarch Job as *"none like him in the earth, a perfect and an upright man, one that feareth God, and escheweth evil"* (Job 1:8), and He defended him against the verbal attacks of his friends, when Job was going through a vicious satanic assault, saying to them, *"Ye have not spoken of me the thing that is right, as my servant Job hath"* (Job 42:7).

Yet when God finally spoke to Job, in Job 38–41, He answered none of Job's questions concerning the reason for his suffering, nor did He answer the wrong accusations of Job's friends. Instead, He gave out a remarkable monologue about His own great creation and its providential maintenance. The monologue took the form of some 70 or more rhetorical questions having to do with that creation and Job's lack of understanding thereof. *"Where wast thou when I laid the foundations of the earth?"* That was his first question; the rest had to do with numerous remarkable phenomena in the physical world and in the biological world — the very phenomena which Adam and his descendants should have been seeking to understand in order truly to subdue the earth, and develop it to the glory of God and the benefit of His creation.

Neither Job nor his friends could answer these questions, yet presumably they (especially Job) were the wisest and most spiritually minded men of their generation. Yet they and their forebears had had some 2,000 years or more to study the problems and learn the answers.

But neither can we, after some 4,000 or more years since Job! If God needed to rebuke Job — not for his wickedness, but for his lack of concern for God's dominion mandate, then what must He say about us? Our vaunted advances in knowledge and civilization are trivial compared to the potential there for us to learn and do in God's great creation.

Even those marvels we have been able to comprehend in science have been encrusted with the ugly veneer of science falsely so-called — that is, evolutionism. And even man's great contributions in the fine arts have been polluted with utter banality and even blasphemy in so much of what now passes for art, music, and literature. The sophisticated realms of economics and business are intermingled with much greed, deception, and even criminality. And true education for transmitting truth has been undermined, so that the real truth as found in Christ and His creation has been submerged in humanistic philosophy.

It would seem, despite our so-called high civilization, we are still far from fulfilling God's dominion mandate. Our beloved United States nation has probably contributed more than any other nation to what *has* been accomplished, but even this is really trivial compared to what we don't know and have not done.

In reference to the command to nations to *"seek the Lord,"* as stipulated in Acts 17:27, there has been at least limited obedience on the part of some nations — Martin Luther's Germany, John Wesley's and Charles Spurgeon's England, and perhaps others, especially the United States and Canada — but, it is doubtful whether today any nation, as a whole, could be described as truly seeking God as revealed in the Bible and in the Lord Jesus Christ. One has to acknowledge this even in America, in spite of many encouraging developments in recent years — the modern creationist revival, the development of many Bible-believing mega-churches, the strong missionary corps, the worldwide radio transmission of biblical truth now taking place, the great proliferation of Christian literature, all largely centered in America. These all are still minority witnesses, however, with seemingly only marginal effects on our nation or its leadership as a whole.

Most of the world's other present-day nations have thus failed almost totally in most aspects of the dominion mandate — especially marriage and family, technology, education, and, most of all, seeking the true God. They may tend to question and complain about God and His ways, just like Job and his friends, but God can justifiably rebuke them even more than He did in Job's situation. One has to sense that the *"times appointed"* for all modern nations must be nearing the end.

Human Governments

Another component of the dominion mandate was given to Noah and his sons following the great flood. All present-day nations are descendants of these men, of course, and so are under this part of the mandate as well.

That component was the authorization of human government of a more comprehensive structure than just that of the father as head of each house. The command was very simple, yet exceedingly broad in its implications. *"Whoso sheddeth man's blood, by man shall his blood be shed"* (Gen. 9:6). The crime of murder was no longer to be merely the trigger of a series of family "payback" revenge killings, leading to general continuing violence, as in the antediluvian world, but was to be punished by execution ordered and carried out by some representative human agency.

But this would inevitably imply the need to exercise some kind of control also over those human activities which might otherwise lead to murder — such things as robbery, assault, slander, rape, etc. In some ways, laws would have to be set up governing human behavior, with appropriate punishment probably short of death for disobedience.

It is significant that God did not command any particular form of government, but just the basic institution of human government. As noted earlier, the earliest such government was probably at Babel, under Nimrod, whose strength and abilities seem to have automatically enabled him to take charge. This was in the region called Shinar, known to secular historians as Sumer. The dispersion then led to local family leaders serving as tribal chieftains and their clans as the people scattered over the world.

Thus, the first form of human government seems to have been one of numerous city-states, each under the rule of its founder and his successors. As these grew, whether by conquest of other such states or just by family expansion, they developed usually into kingdoms or even empires, ruled by a king or emperor and other officers chosen by that ruler.

Over the centuries, many different forms of government have developed in the different nations of the world, ranging from pure democracies to total dictatorships. There have been absolute monarchies, limited monarchies, oligarchies, feudal systems, fascist and communist states, religious theocracies, and others.

Americans generally believe that the governmental system developed by our founding fathers (Washington, Madison, Jefferson, et al.) is the best of all, although this opinion is not necessarily shared by the rest of the world. Nevertheless, many nations have tried to emulate it, at least in part. Although many call our government a democracy, it is really a constitutional republic, with the balance of governmental power not simply based on the decisions of a king or of the majority of the citizens, but divided between three centers of authority — legislative, administrative, and judicial — each exerting checks and limits on the others, and all adhering to the articles of the federal Constitution. Furthermore, both the Constitution and the legal regulations have been largely founded on the English "common law," which in turn was developed mainly as an application of biblical principles centered around the Ten Commandments.

It is significant, however, as noted above, that the Bible does not specify which form of government should be employed, but only that the nations are responsible to govern themselves, with everything developed with capital punishment as the ultimate weapon.

Whatever form the government may take, it is important to remember that *"there is no power but of God: the powers that be are ordained of God."* Consequently, God's will is that *"every soul be subject unto the higher powers"* (Rom. 13:1). This is true regardless of whether that "power" is kind or cruel, ungodly or righteous. When Paul wrote these words, the wicked Nero was emperor of Rome, and

Paul himself was soon to be imprisoned and beheaded by that monster of a man.

Long before, the Babylonian king Nebuchadnezzar had been forced to acknowledge that *"the most High ruleth in the kingdom of men, and giveth it to whomsoever he will, and setteth up over it the basest of men"* (Dan. 4:17). Remember that God told the cruel pharaoh king of Egypt, *"For this cause I raised thee up, for to shew in thee my great power, and that my name may be declared throughout all the earth"* (Exod. 9:16). And Jesus told Pilate, who was about to deliver Him to be crucified, *"Thou couldest have no power at all against me, except it were given thee from above"* (John 19:11).

Even though we Christians are actually citizens of heaven, we are also commanded to be good citizens of our own nation here on earth. *"Put them in mind to be subject to principalities and powers,"* advised Paul to Pastor Titus concerning his flock, *"to obey magistrates, to be ready to every good work"* (Titus 3:1). And Peter said, *"Submit yourselves to every ordinance of man for the Lord's sake: whether it be to the king, as supreme, Or unto governors, as unto them that are sent by him for the punishment of evildoers, and for the praise of them that do well"* (1 Pet. 2:13–14). The Lord Jesus himself said, *"Render therefore unto Caesar the things which are Caesar's; and unto God the things that are God's"* (Matt. 22:21).

Of course, there is a limit. We are to render to God the service He commands, even if Caesar forbids it. *"We ought to obey God rather than men"* (Acts 5:29) was Peter's response to the decree of the council for the disciples to stop preaching about Christ.

In any case, God is clearly still much aware and concerned about the governments of nations, even though they are neither His chosen nation Israel nor His church. These governments are actually, whether they realize it or care, involved in one key phase of the dominion mandate. For the most part, they have fulfilled this role acceptably, at least in preventing the anarchy that prevailed before the Flood, when there were no governments.

However, one concern is that more and more nations have rejected capital punishment, no matter how heinous the murder or other crime. Since this was the very basis for God authorizing human government, this may turn out to be still another measure of how nations have failed to carry out God's dominion mandate, and therefore may soon find their appointed time ending.

No government is perfect, not even that of the United States. It is interesting to note, however, that God has himself described one form of government as superior to all others. That was the biblical theocracy as set forth in the Pentateuch, but never really fully implemented. His evaluation is found in Deuteronomy 4:5–8.

> *Behold, I have taught you statutes and judgments, even as the LORD my God commanded me, that ye should do so in the land whither ye go to possess it. Keep therefore and do them; for this is your wisdom and your understanding in the sight of the nations, which shall hear all these statutes, and say, Surely this great nation is a wise and understanding people. For what nation is so great, who hath God so nigh unto them, as the LORD our God is in all things that we call upon him for? And what nation is there so great, that hath statutes and judgments so righteous, as all this law, which I set before you this day?*

This theocratic government as described by God through Moses would surely have been the best government in all the history of nations if it had ever been truly implemented. People today, even Christians, might recoil at the strictness and severity of God's laws as set forth by Moses. However, it would have definitely assured national righteousness, justice, and general happiness as no other governmental system has ever done.

There is coming a time, however, when the Lord Jesus Christ returns, that He will establish even a better government throughout the earth. This will be discussed in a later chapter.

CHAPTER IX

WITNESS TO THE GENTILES

Although God had called Abraham to form His elect nation, God had by no means forgotten the other nations. Even though each nation as a whole had departed far from the true God, both in belief and behavior, each person in every nation still possessed the image of God (note James 3:9) and could at least in principle be brought to repentance and back to the true faith. The Bible assures us that God would desire *"all men to be saved, and to come unto the knowledge of the truth"* (1 Tim. 2:4), for He *"is not willing that any should perish, but that all should come to repentance"* (2 Pet. 3:9).

As far as most people in the various nations were concerned, God indeed *"gave them up to uncleanness"* and then *"gave them up unto vile affections"* and finally *"gave them over to a reprobate mind"* (Rom. 1:24, 26, 28). He could no longer work with the nations as such, but He cannot fail in His ultimate purpose, and He will eventually establish *"nations of them which are saved"* (Rev. 21:24) in the new earth.

In the meantime, God's heart is still open to any individual man or woman in the rejected nations who truly desire in their hearts to know and obey Him. *"For the eyes of the LORD run to and fro throughout the whole earth, to shew himself strong in the behalf of those whose heart is perfect toward him"* (2 Chron. 16:9). *"In every nation he that feareth him, and worketh righteousness, is accepted with him"* (Acts 10:35).

Even though the great majority in each nation continue in their own ways, God still seeks those whose hearts are open. The sad truth is that almost all individuals in the nations, as well as the nations as a whole, still continued in their rebellious wickedness, as described so poignantly in the tragic summary of Romans 1:20–32.

Nevertheless, they were *"without excuse"* (Rom. 1:20), for God had provided many witnesses to these unbelieving nations. To those open to His witness, it is reasonable to assume that God has somehow provided enough additional light (as He did to Cornelius in Acts 10:34–48) to enable the recipient to believe and be saved. This does *not* mean, however, that they could be saved by faithfulness to their own particular religion, for all these religions were and are satanic deceptions designed to lead people away from the true God. We shall discuss these religions later in this chapter.

The Testimony of the Creation

But exactly what *were* these universal witnesses available to all men and women of all nations and all times? One, of course, was the Bible in the stars, to which we have alluded in chapter III. Although this system has been corrupted by Satan through Nimrod into the false system of astrology, the same star signs (the constellations) are still there in the heavens, essentially unchanged since the beginning. With their repeated suggestions of a coming Savior who would, after suffering and dying himself, destroy the old serpent and provide salvation, the signs might conceivably be correctly understood in some degree by those open to the convicting work of the Holy Spirit. This was quite possibly the case when the wise men understood that one of the stars was indicating the birth of that promised Savior, and thus were constrained to set out on a long journey to find and worship Him (Matt. 2:1–12).

In addition to the star myths, the legends of numerous ethnic groups around the world not only preserve somewhat distorted records of the great flood and the tower of Babel, but also of the Fall and the promise of a coming deliverer. These were often associated also with the star myths. None of these are sufficiently similar to the true record in the Bible as to provide an adequate basis for saving faith, but they do illustrate the fact that there was a long-ago time *"when they knew God"* (Rom. 1:21). It seems at least possible that some who were *really* seeking God (note Heb. 11:6) might discern enough light in these myths and respond positively enough to warrant God sending more light to them. The Bible tells us that, in some ways we may not comprehend, the Lord Jesus Christ is *"the true Light, which lighteth every man that cometh into the world"* (John 1:9).

A very intriguing remnant of the primeval revelation is the almost universal practice of animal sacrifice — in some cultures even human sacrifice. Although these practices are far removed from those prescribed by God in the Mosaic writings for the nation Israel, they may well suggest a vague tribal consciousness of the importance of substitutionary sacrifice in enabling sinful humans to approach a holy God. The methods used in particular cases, often involving some kind of officiating priesthood, were worthless or even harmful to those participating in the sacrifice, but they conceivably could awaken a sense of sinfulness in the minds and hearts of some individuals and thus a real desire to find the true sacrifice and the true way to approach the true God.

Another type of witness can be seen in the creation itself, at least by those with eyes and hearts that are spiritually sensitive. As the Psalmist wrote:

> *The heavens declare the glory of God; and the firmament sheweth his handiwork. Day unto day uttereth speech, and night unto night sheweth knowledge* (Ps. 19:1–2).

If the heavens are declaring the glory of God, then in some sense they are proclaiming Christ, for He is the very *"brightness of his glory"* (Heb. 1:3), and we are also told that God *"hath shined in our hearts, to give the light of the knowledge of the glory of God in the face of Jesus Christ"* (2 Cor. 4:6).

But just how can the heavens preach Christ? One way, already mentioned, is through the stellar constellations as they had originally been used to denote "the gospel in the stars." But in view of Nimrod's corruption of the heavenly prophetic gospel into the false gospel of works through astrology and evolution, it would be rare indeed for anyone in a later generation to discern the true gospel there, or even enough of it to encourage his seeking more light.

However, the mere contemplation of the heavens, with their inestimable beauty and majesty, should impress anyone with awe and wonder at the power of their Creator, especially when combined with the natural amazement engendered by the intricate designs and complex workings of the earth and all its animal and human inhabitants. This should convince anyone of serious mind and open heart that the Creator of all these marvels must be a mighty being of infinite wisdom and ability.

Then, noting the provision of rain to water the earth and fertile ground from which to produce food for all the animals as well as people, of light and warmth from the sun, of gentle breezes, of rivers and oceans, of refreshing sleep at night, the fantastic process of reproduction, and any number of other good things, that person could easily conclude that that mighty Creator was also a being of mercy and goodness, as well as power and wisdom. In the words of Paul the apostle, when preaching to pagans at Lystra, *"He left not himself without witness, in that he did good, and gave us rain from heaven, and fruitful seasons, filling our hearts with food and gladness"* (Acts 14:17).

Of course, one would observe that occasionally there were violent storms as well as gentle breezes, scorching heat and bitter cold, dry deserts as well as fertile plains, suffering and death along with birth and joy, not to mention wars and fightings. Somehow that wise, powerful, merciful God could also be angry and allow pain in His creation. A person without any Bible or revelation could learn much about God merely by observing nature — assuming he was interested in learning about God.

The classic verse that precedes the terrible indictment of the post-Babel apostasy (Rom. 1:21–32) is as follows:

> *For the invisible things of him from the creation of the world are clearly seen, being understood by the things that are made, even his eternal power and Godhead; so that they are without excuse* (Rom. 1:20).

Those attributes of God which cannot be seen directly — His power, wisdom, mercy, etc., as well as His holiness, wrath, etc. — *can* be seen and *should* be seen indirectly, merely by observing and pondering His creation. And it is inexcusable *not* to see, because they are everywhere to be seen by those with seeing minds and hearts.

The classic verse of Romans 1:20 is often cited as evidence of this by Christians, but only in relation to the tremendous size and complexity of God's creation. Actually, there is more to it than just that, though even that is a true and tremendous blessing. But the verse says that *"even his eternal power and Godhead"* are *"clearly seen."* Just how is that?

With reference to God's *"eternal power,"* God is omnipotent, and this has to be evident from the fact that all the mighty stars of heaven (and think of each of them as a *sun* giving out tremendous energy continually, like our sun) had a Creator able to impart their power to them in the first place, and that He has made at least ten million billion billion such suns. And then ponder the fact that they will all eventually burn out, when all their mighty power will be dispersed through space as low-temperature heat. Evolutionists do have notions about how new stars might be formed, but they never have observed such a thing to actually happen. All that astronomers can *observe* happening is stars burning out — sometimes very rapidly in stellar explosions — never do they see new stars appear where none were there before.

In fact, the whole universe is in a state of decay and will eventually die, if present processes continue long enough, and scientists have called this fact the *second law* (the *first law* is the law of conservation of quantity of energy and power; the *second law* is the law of decay or decreasing availability of that energy and power). These laws (or even just the observed fact of universal decay) should make it obvious that the universe and all its mighty sources of power had a beginning; otherwise it would already be dead. It is not creating itself, so the source of its power is not in time — not *temporal power*. Its Creator, therefore, must be one who has *eternal* power. Therefore, God's *"eternal power"* has been *"clearly seen"* *"from the creation of the world."*

And the fact that the Creator must be a personal being, and not just an impersonal power source, is evident from the fact — also common to both science and universal experience — that every effect must have a cause equal to or greater than itself. The Creator of infinite suns each with great power must have had power greater than all — essentially omnipotent. Similarly, the Creator of billions of individual human beings must be a great being himself, greater than all those He has created.

Consequently, it is not presumptuous but realistic to conclude with the Psalmist that *"the fool hath said in his heart, There is no God"* (Ps. 14:1).

It is inexcusable for a rational person not to see God and His eternal power just from the creation alone.

And what about the *"Godhead"* that is, the nature and structure of God? He is an omnipotent person, but He is also a *unique* person in His very character and structure. He is a triune God — Father, Son, and Spirit — one God manifest in three distinct persons. This is hard to comprehend by our finite minds, but is certainly the teaching of Scripture.

Furthermore, this triune nature of the godhead is reflected in the creation in a remarkable way. In fact, the universe is really a tri-universe, of space and time and matter ("matter" which can be understood as the phenomena continually and everywhere taking place in space and time — in other words, a space/matter/time universe). It is also remarkable that each of these three entities — space, matter, and time — is also a triunity. It is not too much to say that the universe which God created is a trinity of trinities, reflecting in a fantastic way the nature of its Creator.

Note that a trinity — a triunity — is not just a system composed of three parts, like the sides of a triangle or the three parts of an egg. A trinity is not a system of three components adding up to the whole, but a system of three components, each of which *is* the whole!

For example, space has three dimensions, each of which pervades the whole space (modern concepts involving more dimensions are just concepts, not reality; the space we live in is three-dimensional, nothing more nor less).

And time is future, present, and past — each of which involves all time. Then there are all the events that occur in space and during time. Every event is tied in with the cause or combination of causes that produced it and with the effect or effects which it then produces. In that sense, everything that happens in the space-time universe is a trinity of cause/event/consequence, each of which is implicit in the other two.

Furthermore, the three components of the universe bear the same sort of relation to each other as the three persons of the godhead bear to each other. Space is the invisible, omnipresent background of all things. Then the events that happen throughout space require space for their manifestation, and thus manifest the reality of space. Those events also require time in order to be experienced and understood.

Each event has its background in space and its meaning interpreted through time. The triune relationship is something like background/manifestation/meaning — or, simply space/matter/time. Note that each is inseparable from the others. The universe is not part space, part time, part matter — but all space, all time, all events happening in space/time.

Thus, God's physical creation is truly a triuniverse, reflecting the nature of the godhead. The Father is the unseen, omnipresent source of all things, the Son manifests the Father to the senses, and the Holy Spirit makes God real in human experience, though He himself is invisible.[1] One can substitute "space," "matter," and "time" in this sentence for "Father," "Son," and "Spirit," and the same sentence still holds.

Thus, the creation does indeed speak of His eternal power and godhead, so that those who deny Him are *"without excuse."*

Some may object that all this is so intangible that no one could be expected to infer these truths just from nature. Few people do so, of course, but the fact remains that it's all *there*, and has always been there, and does not require any training in science or anything else to see it. That is probably why God, through Paul, has said that those who do not see God through His creation are *"without excuse."*

As a matter of fact, even the grace and mercy of God are manifest throughout the creation by the regular triumph of light over darkness when the sun rises each morning, and of life over death whenever spring comes and new life seems to appear everywhere. The birth of a baby, preceded by pain and suffering, reminds us repeatedly that, even though death universally implies God's judgment on a rebellious world, He has also provided new life out of sufferings and possible death of the one who "creates" that new life. As Jesus said, *"A woman when she is in travail hath sorrow, because her hour is come: but as soon as she is delivered of the child, she remembereth no more the anguish, for joy that a man is born into the world"* (John 16:21).

Although, because of sin and God's curse, *"the whole creation groaneth and travaileth in pain together until now"* (Rom. 8:22), even *that* fact is an ever-present witness to the holiness of God, testifying that man and his dominion are now under the chastening hand of God.

---

1 For a more extensive discussion of these matters, the reader can refer to the writer's *Biblical Basis for Modern Science* (Green Forest, AR: Master Books, 2002).

But, since there is also the ongoing witness of life out of death, men ought somehow to sense the ancient promise that the creation some-day *"shall be delivered from the bondage of corruption into the glorious liberty of the children of God"* (Rom. 8:21).

The Moral Testimony

Another type of witness altogether is that of conscience. Although moral and ethical standards have varied from nation to nation in the past — and still do — it is profoundly significant that moral standards of some kind *do exist* in every human society. This is not an attribute of animals, but only of human beings.

Often many of these standards have been formally written down in the form of legal codes by which the societies are governed. But even without a formal code of laws, every person knows that there is a difference between right and wrong, and that it is better to do right than to do wrong. This fact in itself strongly implies that somewhere, some time, there exists a great Judge who will in some way reward the right and punish the wrong. Otherwise, the world could easily descend into anarchy and chaos, as did the world before the Flood. The judging decision may be made by some kind of human governor on the basis of the legal code guiding that government. But if no government or legal code happens to exist at all in a given tribe, say, it is still true that every person has a God-given conscience, guiding him as to right and wrong, and he still will sense that he must some day give an account to the great — though unknown — Judge.

The apostle Paul discussed this situation as follows:

> *For when the Gentiles, which have not the law, do by nature the things contained in the law, these, having not the law, are a law unto themselves: Which shew the work of the law written in their hearts, their conscience also bearing witness, and their thoughts the mean while accusing or else excusing one another; In the day when God shall judge the secrets of men by Jesus Christ according to my gospel* (Rom. 2:14–16).

It is sadly true, however, that most people do not understand that God might be speaking to them through their conscience, so instead of seeking to know Him better, they ignore Him, just as they have ignored the witness of creation. Like the Cretians of the apostolic period, *"even their mind and conscience is defiled"* (Titus 1:15).

Once again, though, there may be some here or there who will realize that the source of the promptings of their conscience could be the unknown Creator and Judge, and sincerely seek to learn about Him. To such, we perhaps may assume that God will somehow send further light which can lead them to salvation. Remember again that *"the eyes of the LORD run to and fro throughout the whole earth"* (2 Chron. 16:9), seeking those who truly desire to learn of Him. *"The true worshippers shall worship the Father in spirit and in truth: for the Father seeketh such to worship him"* (John 4:23). *"To this man will I look,"* the Lord told His prophet, *"even to him that is poor and of a contrite spirit, and trembleth at my word"* (Isa. 66:2).

Whether there have been such people in the Gentile nations who have not had access to the law or the gospel of God, we do not know. We do know that there is no salvation outside of Christ and through believing on God's redemption as accomplished by Him, so we may at least hope that God sends the needed light to any such who have truly sought Him, as He did to Cornelius (Acts 10).

In addition to the law as written in their hearts, we do know that at least some ancient nations did have written law codes that even antedated the Mosaic laws. Many similarities existed in fact, between such laws (the Hittite Code, the Ebla Code, the Babylonian Code of Hammurabi, etc.), but whether these had to some degree been received from God is very doubtful, as there are too many inconsistencies with the Mosaic laws, and their religious background is clearly pagan rather than biblical. But there is something there, and it is conceivable that God might have used even pagan concepts of ethics and morality to awaken the consciences of some to seek fuller knowledge of the true God. Remember that many cultures had retained some traditions of the creation, Fall, Flood, etc., and the Holy Spirit could have used even these to reach some hearts and minds.

The Religions of the Nations

There have been, and still are, many different religions among the nations of the world, and it is a common notion that all these reflect sincere seekers after God, just going about their search in different ways. They are all heading for the same goal, so the opinion goes, but following different ways to get there. As all roads lead to Rome, so all religions lead to heaven.

Nothing, however, could be more lethally wrong than that idea. Jesus said, *"Enter ye in at the strait gate: for wide is the gate, and broad is the way, that leadeth to destruction, and many there be which go in thereat: Because strait is the gate, and narrow is the way, which leadeth unto life, and few there be that find it"* (Matt. 7:13–14). The very path to apostasy which we have been discussing, and which is elaborated so incisively in Romans 1:21–32, is that of replacing the one true religion centered around the God who created all things with some sort of makeshift religion which *"changed the truth of God into a lie, and worshipped and served the creature more than the Creator"* (Rom. 1:25). That same passage makes it clear that those who do this have been *given up* by God. All such religions are *not* just different ways of reaching God. Rather, they are different ways of rebelling against or just ignoring the true God. *"For though there be that are called gods, whether in heaven or in earth, (as there be gods many, and Lords many,) But to us there is but one God, the Father, of whom are all things, and we in him; and one Lord Jesus Christ, by whom are all things, and we by him"* (1 Cor. 8:5–6).

Of all the world's great religions, only three are monotheistic — Islam, Judaism, and Christianity. The orthodox wings of these all believe in special creation by God (Muslims believe Allah is that God, however, rather than the biblical God Jehovah). Buddhism, Taoism, and Confucianism are essentially pantheistic and philosophical rather than theistic, but on the popular level, their pantheism becomes practical polytheism.

The previous chapter dealt with the nation Israel in its formation and early history. The religion of Israel, however, as practiced at present, has departed far from its original state as set forth in the Old Testament, except for its ultra-Orthodox branch. All of the above religions — including even liberal Christianity — have capitulated to modern evolutionism, and some have even adapted to communism. Hinduism, another great religion, largely confined to India, is essentially polytheistic, and thus similar in many respects to the great religions of the past (Egypt, Sumeria, Greece, Rome, etc.).

One vital feature common to all religions of past or present has been their rejection of the Creator God of the Bible and, consequently, their rejection of His incarnation in Christ. All are works-oriented, with salvation (whatever that means to them) attained through ritualism and works. All have opposed the gospel of Christ and His saving grace. But Christ claimed to be God and to provide the only way to salvation and eternal life, demonstrating that claim to be valid by His wonderful resurrection.

The most important of the world's non-Christian religions is Islam. This religion, founded by Mohammed about A.D. 600, is the nearest to Christianity in some respects, yet probably its most intractable opponent. Muslims believe in one God (Allah) and in creation rather than evolution (although there are now many liberals in Islam who do accept evolution). They also believe in the Bible, although they think it has been corrupted by later theologians. They accept the virgin birth of Christ and even His second coming, though they reject His death and resurrection. There are many similarities in the moral teachings of the Bible and their holy book, the Koran, but also many serious differences.

The main difference is that they worship a different god (Allah) than the God of the Bible. The Koran is given, or so it is claimed, by verbal inspiration from Allah, transmitted through the angel Gabriel to the so-called prophet Mohammed (who must really be one of the major false prophets warned about by Christ in Matthew 24:11). Allah is making the claim throughout the Koran that it is he who is dictating its words. These words cannot be coming from the true God, for they contradict the words of the Bible at many, many places. Most seriously, Allah denies that Jesus is the Son of God and that He died for our sins and rose again. Furthermore, Allah instructs Muslims to slay infidels, meaning non-Muslims, if they refuse to become Muslims. Also he instructs them to slay any Muslim who becomes a Christian (and many Muslim nations have such a law and enforce it). Obviously, therefore, Allah cannot possibly be the true God, but rather (like Satan) aspires to take the place of God. There is no salvation in Islam, but only through Jesus Christ. *"Neither is there salvation in any other: for there is none other name under heaven given among men, whereby we must be saved"* (Acts 4:12).

There have been many individuals who have been saved as converts from one of these fake religions, but only when they have come out of it and received Christ. It is possible, of course, that something in their religion constrained them to read the Bible or consult a Christian friend or something, which the Holy Spirit then used to bring them to Christ, but they could not have been saved by remaining in and practicing their false religion, no matter how sincere they may have been. The evidence for the truth of Christ is available if one looks for it, especially in this present age when Bibles and Christian literature are in abundant supply practically everywhere, not to mention all the other types of witness God has provided throughout history.

Gentile Salvation before Christ

We have noted various ways in which God provided a witness to the nations of the world after the dispersion at Babel (through creation, conscience, etc.) before Christ — or even before the call of Israel. We have also speculated — perhaps wistfully hoping — that some people have actually responded to such witness, to the degree that God somehow has sent them enough additional light to enable them to be saved. There have been numerous such cases reported in the missionary literature. Nevertheless, it is true that the vast majority of the people continued blindly and stubbornly in the ways of Nimrod, as described in Romans 1:21–32.

The patriarch Job is a good example of one early non-Israelite who knew God. He apparently lived and served the Lord before Abraham was called to establish a new nation, and was a godly, righteous man, as God himself testified to Satan and all the angels (Job 1:8; 2:3). God also called him *"my servant Job"* when rebuking Job's friends for their unwarranted accusations against Him (Job 42:7). Job had also been faithful in offering sacrifices and was confident that he would one day see God (Job 19:25–26). It is likely that his friends also believed in the true God, though their knowledge of His ways was very incomplete. That all this took place before the nation Israel existed is evident from the fact that Israel is not mentioned anywhere in Job's 42 chapters.

There is, however, a rather cryptic reference to the probability that Job had access to some form of early revelation from God, for he said, *"Neither have I gone back from the commandment of his lips; I have esteemed the words of his mouth more than my necessary food"* (Job 23:12).

Abraham also had some form of early revelation available, for God mentioned to Isaac that *"Abraham obeyed my voice, and kept my charge, my commandments, my statutes, and my laws"* (Gen. 26:5).

Exactly what form this pre-Mosaic law code may have taken, or how widely it was distributed, we are not told. In any case, it was eventually superseded by the giving of the Law of Moses.

Once the nation of Israel was established, with the Mosaic law in place, including the system of sacrifices, then that nation itself became a witness to the other nations. Even though there was almost perpetual conflict between Israel and other nations, there were many proselytes from other countries that joined with the people of God. Even when they left Egypt at their beginning, there was a "mixed multitude" of proselytes that joined with them (Exod. 12:38). It seems unlikely that many of that particular group would join with a mob of fleeing slaves for any reasons other than spiritual, but join they did.

Then one thinks of Reuel, Moses' father-in-law, who was later also called *"Raguel the Midianite"* (Exod. 2:18; Num. 10:29), the same as Jethro, *"the priest of Midian"* (Exod. 3:1), who later joined up with Moses and the Israelites in their exodus, acknowledging that *"the LORD is greater than all gods"* (Exod. 18:11), and becoming an advisor to Moses.

Balaam of Mesopotamia had apparently been a true prophet of God, even receiving the great Messianic prophecy of the *"Star out of Jacob"* (Num. 24:17), until his greed led him away from his calling and he became a false prophet and was finally slain by the Israelites. However, the fact that God actually had a real prophet far off in Mesopotamia at least suggests that He may have had similar witnesses in other lands, and they certainly must have had some disciples and converts from those lands.

Although the Israelites were at fault for not ridding the Promised Land of the Canaanites, there later were a number of people among those and other pagan tribes who did come to know the Lord because of the witness of Israel.

There was godly young Ruth the Moabitess, for example, who actually entered the ancestral line of King David (Ruth 1:16; 4:22). David himself had a number of *"mighty men"* in his entourage, among whom were *"Zelek the Ammonite"* and *"Uriah the Hittite"* (2 Sam. 23:37, 39). One wonders whether Zelek was the father of *"Naamah an*

Ammonitess" who was Solomon's first wife (almost certainly the woman he loved and wrote about in his Song of Solomon) and the mother of Rehoboam (2 Chron. 12:13), the son who succeeded him as king. The temple was built by Solomon on a site purchased by David from a Jebusite (2 Sam. 24).

And don't forget the remarkable story of the prophet Jonah, whose preaching led the whole city of Assyrian Nineveh to repentance and faith in the true God. There also was Daniel's testimony to the Babylonian Nebuchadnezzar and the Persian Darius, both of whom were led at least to acknowledge the supremacy of God.

It is thus evident that, even though God had called Abraham, and Israel became the chosen nation, He had certainly not forgotten the other nations of the world.

Nor had they completely forgotten Him, though they had rebelled against Him as far as the nations as a whole were concerned. Many scholars have shown, in their ethnological research, that the ancient nations, almost without exception, continued for a long time to recognize His existence. The ancient Sumerians, the early Egyptians, the first Aryans in India, the founding dynasties of China, continued to acknowledge a "high God," who was believed to be essentially unreachable, even while their people as a whole were becoming pantheistic and polytheistic in their day-to-day religion.

Even the so-called primitive animalistic tribes in Africa, the Americas, and the South Seas have recognized a high God, although their daily activities and worship generally center around the spirits.

God has never left himself without witness, as Paul told the pagans at Lystra (Acts 14:17), and He is *"not far from every one of us"* as he told the pagans at Athens (Acts 17:27). There have indeed been at least a few here and there in the Gentile world throughout the ages who have responded to the dim light they had until God sent a Peter or a Jonah or some other light-bearer to bring them more light.

But now the greatest witness and the greatest Light — in fact, the very *"light of the world"* (John 8:12) — has come into the world to provide the way to God, demonstrate and preach the truth of God, and impart the eternal life of God (John 14:6), to all who will believe and receive Him.

CHAPTER X

JUDGMENTS ON THE NATIONS

N ot only is God's ongoing concern with the nations evidenced by His many ways of witness to them, but so is it shown by His repeated corrective judgments on them — which, in fact, is actually another form of witness. God has not allowed them to become too comfortable in their rebellion, but has repeatedly sought to awaken them to repentance. Occasionally, He has sent a human preacher to them (as Jonah to Nineveh), but more frequently He has spoken to them in terms of calamities of one type or another — sometimes invasion by a hostile nation, sometimes by famine, flood, earthquake, or pestilence.

A key verse in this context is Isaiah 45:7, which is as follows: *"I form the light, and create darkness: I make peace, and create evil: I the LORD do all these things."*

It should be obvious that any evil created by God cannot be moral evil, *"for God cannot be tempted with evil, neither tempteth he any man"* (James 1:13). Rather the term is used here, as it often is elsewhere, to refer to physical catastrophes inflicted on a nation by God — such as the ten plagues sent on ancient Egypt and its emperor Pharaoh, in judgment on that nation's treatment of the Israelites.

That the term "evil" is frequently used in this sense is evident from many such passages as in the following typical examples:

Shall there be evil in a city, and the LORD *hath not done it?* (Amos 3:6).

Bring upon them the day of evil, and destroy them with utter destruction (Jer. 17:18).

Actually the word for "evil" (Hebrew *ra*) is translated many different ways, depending on context. It often does denote moral wickedness, but it also refers frequently to one or another type of physical calamity, unpleasantness, or judgment that is being visited upon an entire nation because of its national sinfulness, often serving also as an example and warning to others.

Forms of Divine Rebuke

We are not dealing here with the sufferings that are experienced by individual believers. It is true that some of these may be closely related to a particular sin (e.g., a Christian being sent to prison for shady business dealings), but many (perhaps most) times when believers suffer, there is a higher purpose involved.

It may be for testimonial reasons, as in the case of the sufferings of Job, whose patience and faithfulness were being thereby demonstrated both to Job's friends and also to the principalities and powers in the heavens. It may be for the purpose of generating growth in Christlikeness in the life of His followers. As Paul said, *"Most gladly therefore will I rather glory in my infirmities, that the power of Christ may rest upon me. Therefore I take pleasure in infirmities, in reproaches, in necessities, in persecutions, in distresses for Christ's sake: for when I am weak, then am I strong"* (2 Cor. 12:9–10).

There can be various good reasons for the apparently undeserved sufferings of the righteous. And, of course the greatest example is that of Christ himself, without whose substitutionary death and resurrection there would be no salvation for anyone.

Not so with nations, however, as far as the biblical record is concerned. When catastrophe befalls a nation, God is speaking in judgment, no matter how its leaders and apologists may try to rationalize it away. Again note Amos 3:6. *"Shall there be evil in a city, and the* LORD *hath not done it?"*

Biblical examples are far more abundant than can be expounded in these pages. We shall discuss briefly just a few of them as more or less typical.

One example is that of a physical catastrophe such as an earthquake or flood or storm. For instance, the intolerably wicked cities of the plain, especially Sodom and Gomorrah, were destroyed completely by what seems to have been a great volcanic eruption accompanied by a violent earthquake. *"Lo, the smoke of the country went up as the smoke of a furnace"* (Gen. 19:28).

As another spectacular example, when the armies of five city-states of the Amorites joined together to fight the Israelites at the battle of Beth-horon, *"The LORD cast down great stones from heaven . . . and . . . they were more which died with hailstones than they whom the children of Israel slew with the sword"* (Josh. 10:11). The iniquity of the great Amorite coalition of kingdoms was finally *"full"* (note Gen. 15:16), and this battle marked the effective end of their rule over the Promised Land.

One is tempted, in view of such biblical prototypes, to conclude that devastating catastrophes not mentioned in the Bible, such as the volcanic destructions of Pompeii in Italy and St. Pierre in Martinique, and even the awful hurricane at Galveston and the devastating earthquake at San Francisco in the early years of the 20th century might well have been used as messages from God. These were all natural phenomena, with perfectly adequate scientific explanations, but God does control the systems He created, and introspection is at least warranted when such things "happen."

Other natural calamities such as droughts and famines have also on occasion been used by the Lord as judgmental or warning messages. *"He turneth rivers into a wilderness, and the watersprings into a thirsty ground: A fruitful land into barrenness, for the wickedness of them that dwell therein"* (Ps. 107:33–34).

More than once the Lord sent a famine upon His own special nation Israel because of their sinfulness. In the days of Elijah the prophet, God sent 3½ years of drought in the northern kingdom of Israel because of their wickedness, especially centered in King Ahab and Queen Jezebel. This judgment was not on a Gentile nation, of course, but did show quite clearly that the processes that determine the weather are subject to God's control, so that both abnormal floods and abnormal droughts can be used by Him as instruments of judgment or warning for a nation. In the days of the wicked Claudius Caesar, God sent a famine (as predicted by a prophet named Agabus) that extended throughout the entire empire (see Acts 11:28).

Another form of judgment on nations, both Israel and her enemies, was in the form of pestilence. In a warning to Israel, God said, *"The Lord shall smite thee with a consumption, and with a fever, and with an inflammation, and with an extreme burning, and with the sword, and with blasting, and with mildew; and they shall pursue thee until thou perish"* (Deut. 28:22). When the ark of the covenant had been taken by the Philistines, the people of the land were afflicted in their bodies, and so were the Egyptians when they refused to let the Israelites go.

One cannot help but think of the modern plague of AIDS, afflicting the people of many nations today, including America; the sins of sexual perversion, including homosexuality, have been present throughout history, but today such perversions are being both defended and widely promoted as a respectable lifestyle by intellectuals and political leaders, even by many religious spokesmen. There is clearly a cause-and-effect relation between AIDS and sodomy — as well as sexual immorality and sexually transmitted diseases in general. It is not at all far-fetched to think that this new epidemic could be a modern visitation from God as a judgment because of the explosive spread of this old sin.

Undoubtedly, the Bible's most frequently mentioned judgments on nations have to do with invasions by hostile armies. We have referred previously to the termination of God's appointed times for various nations that had failed to fulfill God's purpose in raising them up. Frequently such termination was accomplished by this particular means, as one ungodly nation invaded and destroyed or subjugated another, only to be in turn subjected to rejection and defeat herself. We have already noted some of the most notorious such instances. Babylonia was defeated by Persia, then Persia by Greece, and Greece by Rome. The old Roman Empire was invaded by various nations they considered barbarians and replaced in some degree by the so-called Holy Roman Empire, the Roman Catholic Church and its pope.

Then that "empire," in turn, while still powerful, lost much of its power and prestige to various European nations as a result of the Renaissance and especially the Protestant Reformation. Even before that, the Church split into two branches, one centered at Rome, the other at Constantinople. The latter became the center of several so-called Orthodox churches, the most influential being the Greek Orthodox, also known as Byzantine (after Byzantium, the earlier name of Constantinople, now Istanbul).

These organizations, and the nations that came out of them, are still in existence, so perhaps the Lord is not yet finished with them, though none are as powerful and influential as they have been in the past from time to time. We should note that all are still at least nominally committed to the God of the Bible. Some, at least, are still actively involved in science, business, and other aspects of improving the world under God's dominion mandate, even though that purpose is not their motivation. Whatever the mind of God may be toward them, they still survive.

The Non-Christian Nations

But what about those many nations that are not even nominally believers in the true God of creation and His Son, Jesus Christ? The Moslem nations especially are numerous and powerful, and the Muslim people are becoming more widespread all the time. There are also Hindu nations (India), Buddhist nations (Thailand, Laos, etc.), Shintoist nations (Japan), etc.

The world's largest nation in population is China. Although its Christian minority is growing, its roots are a combination of Buddhism, Taoism, and Confucianism, with atheistic communism now more or less the official religion. The non-Moslem African nations, still largely animist, in some cases now have largely nominally Christian populations. Islam is also growing rapidly in Africa.

China is an enigma in many ways. So is India, which is also very old, very large, and very heavily populated. For some reason, God has been unusually long-suffering with these two nations (as well as others) in terms of their times appointed and their boundaries of habitation.

Both have long been pagan nations as a whole, but there are considerable indications that, in their earliest histories, their ancestors did have faith in the true God of heaven. Similarly, there are indications that early Christian missionaries conducted successful ministries in both countries. In modern times, great numbers have become Christians in both nations, though the nations as a whole remain antagonistic to the gospel. Also, each nation is made up of many sub-nations, each with its own language and ethnicity. The histories are long and complex, and individually diverse characteristics emerge when each sub-nation is studied as a separate entity. No doubt, the rise and fall of these tribal units would provide a challenging study to discern God's particular dealings with them.

This has also been true of many of the Moslem nations, although some — like Egypt and Arabia — do have long histories of their own. Of course, ancient Hamitic Egypt is now mostly a Semitic Arab state, and Arabia is notable as the birthplace of Mohammed and the Muslim religion. Whether these facts had a bearing on God's long patience with Egypt, Arabia, and other Arab states is only a guess. Whatever else Islam is, it is certainly monotheistic, making much of Mohammed's conviction that there is only one God, the God who created all things, demanding that men worship Him only. Whether Allah and Jehovah are really just two names for the one God is another question altogether, however, and we have already shown, in fact, that they are not. Allah is a false god desiring to be worshiped as the true God. Perhaps, instead of being just another name for God, Allah is really just another name for Satan!

It is speculative, however, to attempt to discern reasons why God has, or has not, judged a certain nation for its sins except in those instances where He had actually given a specific reason in Scripture. There are a number of cases where this information is specifically given, and these can be used as partial clues as to His reasons for dealing with others.

For instance, the judgments against the ancient nations Ammon, Moab, Edom, and Philistia were at least in major part due to their hatred of Israel. Against Ammon, God said, *"Because thou hast clapped thine hands, and stamped with the feet, and rejoiced in heart with all thy despite against the land of Israel . . . I . . . will deliver thee for a spoil to the heathen . . . and thou shalt know that I am the LORD"* (Ezek. 25:6–7). For the same basic reason, God said,

"I will execute judgments upon Moab; and they shall know that I am the Lord" (Ezek. 25:11).

To Edom, descended from Jacob's own brother but an inveterate enemy of Israel, the judgment was this: *"Because that Edom hath dealt against the house of Judah . . . And I will lay my vengeance upon Edom by the hand of my people Israel"* (Ezek. 25:12–14). The Philistines likewise. *"I will execute great vengeance upon them with furious rebukes; and they shall know that I am the"Lord"* (Ezek. 25:17).

That justifying phrase, *"Thou shalt know that I am the Lord,"* occurs in judgment upon nations opposing Israel and denying God no less than 60 times just in the Book of Ezekiel. It can be a dangerous thing indeed for a nation to come to the point of actually denying as a nation that the true and only God of creation is *"the Lord"* — that is — *Jehovah.* The Psalmist has reminded us that *"the wicked shall be turned into hell, and all the nations that forget God"* (Ps. 9:17). That, apparently, is the greatest sin of all — that of finally repudiating and forgetting the God who made them.

The classic example of a nation receiving punishment from God at the hands of another nation more wicked than itself, of course, is that of God's elect nation Israel being defeated and carried away captive by the Assyrians and Babylonians.

The prophet Hosea prophesied mainly against the apostate wickedness of the ten-tribe northern kingdom of Israel during its terminal years, saying, *"Samaria shall become desolate; for she hath rebelled against her God"* (Hos. 13:16). Samaria, of course, was the capital of the northern kingdom. This prophetic judgment was soon fulfilled when the Assyrian armies swept over the land. *"Then the king of Assyria came up throughout all the land, and went up to Samaria, and besieged it three years. In the ninth year of Hoshea the king of Assyria took Samaria, and carried Israel away into Assyria . . ."* (2 Kings 17:5–6).

This was done only after much exhortation by Hosea, Isaiah, Micah, and other prophets to Israel to repent and return to the Lord. *"Yet the Lord testified against Israel . . . by all the prophets . . . saying, Turn ye from your evil ways . . . Notwithstanding they would not hear, but hardened their necks. . . . Therefore the Lord was very angry with Israel, and removed them out of his sight. . . . So was Israel carried away out of their own land to Assyria unto this day"* (2 Kings 17:13–23).

And so the ten tribes became the famous "ten lost tribes of Israel," because they never returned as a nation back to the Promised Land. Not all the individuals in the ten tribes were lost, for some had migrated back to Judah — both before and after the Assyrian exile, becoming part of the Jewish nation. But the ten tribes as a whole never returned — a tragic ending for most of God's chosen nation.

As far as the remaining tribes were concerned (Judah and Benjamin, along with many Levites and Simeonites, and a scattering from the others who had migrated back toward Jerusalem) this kingdom, called Judah, survived another hundred or so years.

However, except for a few years of partial revival under such good kings as Hezekiah and Josiah, the people of Judah soon had departed from God and His laws just as the northern Israelites had done. Jeremiah warned repeatedly that God's judgment was imminent, but received nothing but persecution for his efforts. Among other warnings, he sounded forth the following: *"Lo, I will bring a nation upon you from far, O house of Israel, saith the Lord: it is a mighty nation, it is an ancient nation . . . Their quiver is an open sepulcher, they are all mighty men. . . . They shall impoverish thy fenced cities, wherein thou trustedst, with the sword"* (Jer. 5:15–17).

The nation of which Jeremiah warned was, of course, the great Babylonian empire, the oldest of them all (in the form of Babel, the rebellious city of Nimrod). The reason for this imminent invasion and destruction was the accumulated wickedness and idolatry of Jerusalem and the whole nation of Judah.

> *For the children of Judah have done evil in my sight, saith the Lord: they have set their abominations in the house which is called by my name, to pollute it . . . to burn their sons and their daughters in the fire . . . Therefore, behold the days come, saith the Lord . . . will I cause to cease from the cities of Judah, and from the streets of Jerusalem, the voice of mirth, and the voice of gladness . . . for the land shall be desolate* (Jer. 7:30–34).

The Book of Jeremiah is replete with dire prophecies of the devastation destined to fall on Judah and Jerusalem, because of their evil deeds, especially rebelling against God. The day came when all were fulfilled. *"Therefore [God] brought upon them the king of the Chaldees, who slew their young men with the sword in the house of their sanctuary . . . And they burnt the house of God, and brake down the wall of Jerusalem . . . And them that had escaped from the sword carried he away to Babylon . . ."* (2 Chron. 36:17–20).

That was not the end of God's purpose in calling Israel, of course, for He cannot fail. Assyria and Babylonia had been instruments in God's hand to chastise His children, as it were, but they were worse than the ones being punished, and their time was coming. *"The LORD hath raised up the spirit of the kings of the Medes: for his device is against Babylon, to destroy it; because it is the vengeance of the LORD, the vengeance of his temple. . . . O thou that dwellest upon many waters, abundant in treasures, thine end is come, and the measure of thy covetousness"* (Jer. 51:11–13). We have already referred to the fall of Babylon, when the Medes and Persians suddenly and unexpectedly invaded the city and ended the time of her habitation.

Cruel and wicked Assyria, with her vile capital, Nineveh, also came to a sudden and violent end, as predicted by the prophet Nahum. *"Woe to the bloody city! it is all full of lies and robbery . . . There is no healing of thy bruise; thy wound is grievous: all that hear the bruit of thee shall clap the hands over thee: for upon whom hath not thy wickedness passed continually?"* (Nah. 3:1–19).

Assyria's final defeat was accomplished at the Battle of Carshemesh, being accomplished by a combined army of Chaldeans, Medes, and Scythians.

In the meantime, both Babylonia and Assyria had been used by God to punish many other wicked nations that had similarly squandered their God-given opportunities. One after another, the post-Babel nations had miserably failed. Some had made worthwhile contributions to the accomplishment of God's dominion mandate to *"subdue the earth,"* but even these had been with the wrong motivation. And none had truly sought after the true God. All had followed one form or another of evolutionism (either atheistic or pantheistic), seeking to account for the universe and all its systems and inhabitants by some means other than special creation by the self-existent God.[1]

---

1 See the writer's treatise, *The Long War Against God* (Green Forest, AR: Master Books, 1989), for full documentation of this fact.

God had not left himself without witness to the nations, of course, even though He had called out Israel as a special nation to himself, for the implementing of His major purpose of redemption for the world. We can hope that at least some individual seekers of God had been brought to himself as a result of this witness during the various ages from the many pagan nations. But most, if not all, are lost forever.

CHAPTER XI

THE MISSIONARY MANDATE

As we have noted, God's chosen nation Israel has been suffering His chastening hand ever since most of her people rejected their Messiah, even pressuring their Roman overlords to have Him crucified. Thus, these are still *"the times of the Gentiles"* (Luke 21:24), as indeed they have been ever since the Assyrians and Babylonians carried the Israelites into captivity several hundred years before Messiah came (2 Kings 17:18; 25:21).

At the same time, none of this really caught God by surprise. *"Known unto God are all his works from the beginning of the world"* (Acts 15:18). As James, the early church leader in Jerusalem, said, *"God at the first* [that is, 'for the first time'] *did visit the Gentiles, to take out of them a people for his name"* (Acts 15:14).

The Holy Spirit is now building a new sort of nation called *"the church of God"* (Paul speaks of three great "nations" — the Jews, the Gentiles, and the church of God — see 1 Cor. 10:32). Members of that new "nation" can be either Jews or Gentiles, of course, but all are *"fellowcitizens with the saints, and of the household of God. . . . In whom ye also are builded together for an habitation of God through the Spirit"* (Eph. 2:19–22).

Note that they are being *"taken out"* of the Gentile world, to be united with those of the chosen people — here called *"the saints"* — who have received Christ. Together, they form *"the church of God"*; in fact, the Greek word translated "church" itself means "those called out."

But just *how* are they being called out of the Gentiles to join with those Jews (Paul, Peter, etc.) who *have* accepted Christ as their Messiah and, more importantly, as their personal Savior from sin?

The Spirit of God is calling them, of course, but He is working in and through the human disciples of Christ — whether Jew or Gentile by nationality — to do so. In fact, this is an actual command of God to every one who becomes His disciple — that is, to *"preach the gospel to every creature"* (Mark 16:15).

This is the second great global mandate given by the Lord. The first mandate was to all those created in God's image, given to Adam and Eve at the very beginning of human history.

The second mandate is given to each person who becomes *"a new creature"* in Christ (2 Cor. 5:17). It was first given at the beginning of *Christian* history, to the disciples of Christ and not intended for the mass of mankind in general.

Both mandates are still in effect. The first is the dominion mandate (Gen. 1:26, 28), often called also "the cultural mandate" (especially by theological liberals). It has been discussed especially in chapters II and V. The second mandate is directed only to Christian disciples, but applies to every nation in its ministration.

The Great Commission

What is called the missionary mandate in this chapter is identified by most Christians as the "great commission," whereby Christ told His first disciples to spread the good news about His sacrificial death and victorious resurrection, with their assurance of salvation and everlasting life, to people in every nation. The Lord Jesus Christ stressed this command at least five different times, as recorded in all four gospels and in the Book of Acts, expressing it in different ways each time.

During His earthly ministry of teaching to His disciples, He once sent them out on a sort of short-term training mission, but only sent them to witness to other Jews. As He sent them out, He said:

> *Go not into the way of the Gentiles . . . But go rather to the lost sheep of the house of Israel* (Matt. 10:5–6).

At that time they could not preach about His death and resurrection, which were yet future, but rather they were told to *"preach, saying, The kingdom of heaven is at hand"* (Matt. 10:7).

On that first occasion, only the first 12 disciples were sent out. Later, he sent 70 disciples out on a similar mission, again apparently just to the cities where He himself planned to preach (note Luke 10:1). At that time, He hinted that this missionary enterprise would soon be expanded, saying:

> *The harvest truly is great, but the labourers are few: pray ye therefore the Lord of the harvest, that he would send forth labourers into his harvest* (Luke 10:2).

That the purpose of Christ already extended beyond just the nation of Israel, however, is evident from His preaching in Samaria, first to the Samaritan woman at the well, then to the many Samaritans who came out later to hear Him (John 4:39–42), even though He had told her plainly that up to that point in time, at least, *"salvation is of the Jews"* (John 4:22).

On that occasion, while the woman had gone into the city to tell the other Samaritans about her encounter with Christ, the Lord told His disciples:

> *Lift up your eyes, and look on the fields; for they are white already to harvest. And he that reapeth receiveth wages, and gathereth fruit unto life eternal: that both he that soweth and he that reapeth may rejoice together* (John 4:35–36).

Clearly, the Lord was preparing His disciples for their future lifelong ministry of witnessing, preaching the gospel, and soul-winning. In fact, when He first chose the 12, He had told them, *"Come ye after me, and I will make you to become fishers of men"* (Mark 1:17).

That He was also concerned about the Gentiles, as well as the Jews and Samaritans, is evident from His reference to God's provision for the widow woman in Sidon and the healing of Naaman of Syria, back during the ministries of Elijah and Elisha (Luke 4:25–27). He also once traveled out of Israel into the Syrophoenician cities of Tyre and Sidon, where he healed the daughter of a Greek woman living there (see Mark 7:24–26), commenting on her great faith. Similarly, when he healed the servant of a Roman centurion, He said, *"I have not found so great faith, no, not in Israel"* (Matt. 8:10).

All of the above incidents took place before He actually paid the price on the cross for our (and their) salvation. Once that was accomplished, however, and following His resurrection, He began explicitly giving their Great Commission — their worldwide missionary mandate.

First of all, when He first appeared after His resurrection to His disciples in the upper room, He said to them:

Peace be unto you: as my Father hath sent me, even so send I you (John 20:21).

This command in itself was not yet very explicit as to where they were being sent or what they were to do there. But then, just a few days later, apparently on a mountain in Galilee, He told the 11 disciples:

All power is given unto me in heaven and in earth. Go ye therefore, and teach all nations, baptizing them in the name of the Father, and of the Son, and of the Holy Ghost: Teaching them to observe all things whatsoever I have commanded you: and, lo, I am with you always, even unto the end of the world. Amen (Matt. 28:18–20).

Not just Israel and Samaria, or even adding Greece and Rome, but *all* nations! *That* is where He was sending them! The word "nations," of course (Greek *ethnos*), is also translated elsewhere as "Gentiles" or "heathen"; either of which would also fit the context. In any case, the command is clearly to go to all the Gentile nations, preaching and teaching the saving and living gospel of Christ.

Luke, in his gospel, indicated also that (as had John's account) the Commission had first been given in the upper room, probably at His first post-resurrection appearance to the assembled disciples.

Thus it is written, and thus it behoved Christ to suffer, and to rise from the dead the third day: And that repentance and remission of sins should be preached in his name among all nations, beginning at Jerusalem. And ye are witnesses of these things (Luke 24:46–48).

Thus, not only were they to go to all the nations, but the preaching was especially to focus on His atoning death and resurrection, as the basis for forgiveness, and repentance evidencing true faith in the person and work of Christ.

Then, there was Mark's report of the Commission being given very succinctly, seemingly just before Christ's departure back into heaven:

> *Go ye into all the world, and preach the gospel to every creature. He that believeth and is baptized shall be saved; but he that believeth not shall be damned* (Mark 16:15–16).

In Mark's account, belief is stressed. In Luke's, it was repentance. Actually, each implies the other. *"Repentance toward God, and faith toward our Lord Jesus Christ"* (Acts 20:21) is the way Paul expressed it. As far as baptism is concerned, true saving faith will be inevitably followed by a willingness and desire to testify to that faith by baptism, but Christ said only that *"he that believeth not"* (not, "he that is not baptized") would be condemned. The Lord Jesus had also told Nicodemus (who probably had witnessed the baptisms taking place in Jordan) that:

> *He that believeth on him is not condemned: but he that believeth not is condemned already, because he hath not believed in the name of the only begotten Son of God* (John 3:18).

There is one more very remarkable statement of this missionary mandate, given by the Lord Jesus just immediately prior to His ascension.

> *But ye shall receive power, after that the Holy Ghost is come upon you: and ye shall be witnesses unto me both in Jerusalem, and in all Judea, and in Samaria, and unto the uttermost part of the earth* (Acts 1:8).

Here, the Commission is not only a command but also a prophecy. "Ye *shall* be . . ." Jesus said.

Consider the apparent absurdity of such a prophecy. Here is a wandering country preacher, with no education and with no travel experience of any consequence, presuming to say that his motley group of unimpressive followers would get His unpalatable message of repentance and His impossible claim of rising from the dead preached all over the world. Absolute nonsense! Who could possibly believe them?

But the amazing fact is that this "impossible" prophecy is a *fulfilled* prophecy! His message has, indeed, been proclaimed and echoed in every nation, and millions upon millions have believed it and had their lives transformed by it, and gone to heaven because of it! As the centurion who watched Him die on the cross was constrained to admit:

> *Truly this was the Son of God* (Matt. 27:54).

The Apostles and the Great Commission

There is no doubt that the Apostles took Christ's missionary mandate literally and seriously, although at first they stayed in Jerusalem. Thousands of Jews, who knew beyond question that Christ was alive again, accepted Him, were baptized, and became part of that first local church. Many other converts, having been in Jerusalem when the Holy Spirit fell on them at the Feast of Pentecost but who lived in other nations, no doubt returned home spreading the gospel message in their home countries (from Persia to Mesopotamia to Libya to Rome and elsewhere — see Acts 2:9–11).

Then, when persecution began in Jerusalem, *"they that were scattered abroad went every where preaching the word"* (Acts 8:4). Philip preached in Samaria, later won a prominent official on his way back home to Ethiopia, and then went on to various other cities. Peter, in the meantime, had been sent by God to an Italian centurion named Cornelius, whose whole household was converted when Peter told them about Christ. They were indeed scattered everywhere, preaching the word. According to extra-biblical traditions, Thomas eventually went to India, Bartholomew to Parthia, Andrew to Scythia, James the Less to Egypt, Thaddeus to Mesopotamia, John to Asia Minor, and Philip to Phrygia. Peter may have gone to Rome (according to the Catholics at least), but he actually wrote one of his epistles from Babylon (1 Pet. 5:13). James, the brother of John, was executed by Herod while still in Jerusalem. Little is known about Simon the Zealot but, since Jesus chose him, one can assume that he also had a significant missionary ministry. The same is true of Matthew, although one tradition has him in Ethiopia.

Luke, the author of the Gospel of Luke and also the Book of Acts, apparently accompanied Paul on his extensive missionary travels. Mark accompanied Paul on his first missionary journey, then went with Barnabas, but seems also to have been closely associated with Peter, especially in the writing of his own gospel. James and Jude, the human brothers of Christ, each wrote one of the New Testament epistles, but little is known of their travels. James seems to have stayed in Jerusalem as head of the church there, where he was eventually martyred. In fact, all of the Apostles eventually became martyrs, with the exception of John, who lived to a good old age. For a while he was imprisoned on the Isle of Patmos, and may have died in Ephesus.

The epistles of Paul and the others were written to Christians rather than to potential converts. However, they all clearly reveal the missionary zeal of the writers.

Most of those to whom Paul wrote had, in fact, been people whom he had won to the Lord in his travels, and he encouraged them also to be true witnesses. An exception was his letter to Rome, since he had not yet been there when he wrote. However, he said that his hope when he reached Rome was to *"have some fruit among you also, even as among other Gentiles"* (Rom. 1:13). He did, indeed, do just that, although he had to do his preaching as a prisoner under house arrest (Acts 28:30–31) to those who came to see him there.

To the Corinthians, Paul wrote, *"I am made all things to all men, that I might by all means save some"* (1 Cor. 9:22). To the Thessalonians, all of whom he had led to Christ, he wrote, *"For what is our hope, or joy, or crown of rejoicing? Are not even ye in the presence of our Lord Jesus Christ at his coming? For ye are our glory and joy"* (1 Thess. 2:19–20). And to Timothy, whom he called *"my own son in the faith"* (1 Tim. 1:2), he wrote, urging him to *"do the work of an evangelist"* (2 Tim. 4:5), even though he knew Timothy already had many other pastoral duties.

Peter urged the Christian wives of non-Christian husbands to live in such a winsome way, wearing the *"ornament of a meek and quiet spirit"* that their husbands might *"without the word be won by the conversation of the wives"* (1 Pet. 3:1–4). He urged all his readers to *"be ready always to give an answer to every man that asketh you a reason of the hope that is in you with meekness and fear"* (1 Pet. 3:15).

Finally, John, whose gospel was written *"that ye might believe that Jesus is the Christ, the Son of God; and that believing ye might have life through his name"* (John 20:31), wrote also of that future time when *"a great multitude . . . of all nations, and kindreds, and people, and tongues"* will stand before the Lamb on His throne, praising Him for their salvation (Rev. 7:9).

In summary, all those first Apostles and the writers of the New Testament, as well as the leaders of the apostolic church in general, did whatever they could to spread the gospel of Christ to all the other nations, even though they themselves were all Jews. As Paul wrote, *"The gospel of Christ . . . is the power of God unto salvation . . . to the Jew first, and also to the Greek"* (Rom. 1:16).

There are even some indications that the gospel penetrated into China at a very early time, as well as all over Europe. It certainly reached England and Ireland in the first century. The apparent claim of Colossians 1:23 to the effect that the gospel *"was preached to every creature which is under heaven"* may not have been precisely translated, because it is very doubtful that it had been preached to the American Indians or the South Sea islanders during Paul's lifetime. The phrase "to every creature" could, in fact, be alternatively translated as "in every creation," and this concept is true. The power, wisdom, grace, and love of God can indeed be seen throughout all creation, by those with eyes to see (Ps. 19:1; Rom. 1:20; etc.).

In any case, there have been Christians who have continued to carry the message of salvation through Christ everywhere century after century, sometimes only being preached in its purity by small persecuted sects. It began to grow rapidly once again after the printing press and the Reformation. The modern missionary movement is believed to have begun when the Baptist pioneer William Carey of England went to India some 200 years ago.

The "nation" called *"the church of God"* (1 Cor. 10:32) has, during the 20 centuries since God first began to *"visit the Gentiles, to take out of them a people for his name"* (Acts 15:14), fragmented into many divisions — denominations, sects, and even pseudo-Christian cults, as well as many para-church organizations.

Christianity is now the largest religion in the world, supposedly, with about two billion professing Christians, one-third of the world's population. However, less than half of those could be considered Bible-believing, committed disciples of Christ; some would argue that the number is less than ten percent, but only God knows. In any case, there is obviously still work to be done, with billions still unreached with the saving gospel of Christ.

The missionary mandate indicates that the aim is for the gospel to be preached to every creature (Mark 16:15). This is not possible, how-ever, since multitudes have already died without hearing it. More real-istic is the call to teach *"all nations,"* even to *"the uttermost part of the earth"* (Matt. 28:19; Acts 1:8). This was a very comprehensive commis-sion, yet not impossible to achieve, and Christian missionaries, radio, television, literature, and other means have been used effectively in try-ing to accomplish it, for many years now.

But it is still unfinished. In His great prophetic discourse on the Mount of Olives just a few days before His crucifixion, the Lord men-tioned a number of signs that would characterize future world history (wars, false prophets, etc.). But when referring to His triumphant re-turn in power, He made one key prediction:

> *And this gospel of the kingdom shall be preached in all the world for a witness unto all nations; and then shall the end come* (Matt. 24:14).

Mark's account of this prophecy simply says that *"the gospel must first be published among all nations"* (Mark 13:10). Remember also that Jesus said just before His ascension that *"ye shall be witnesses unto me . . . unto the uttermost part of the earth"* (Acts 1:8).

These statements seem to tell us clearly that not necessarily every individual will be reached but that every nation (Greek *ethnos* — that is, ethnic group) must have at least a meaningful witness about the gos-pel before Christ returns, so that finally there will be representatives in heaven *"of all nations, and kindreds, and people, and tongues"* (Rev. 7:9). This is surely a great incentive to do all we can to get the gospel out to those who have never heard it, for we can never know (nor could any generation before us have known) whether that very last linguistic group would be finally hearing it during their particular generation.

It does seem, however, that we must be *very* near that time right now. We should surely be doing all we can to be *"hasting unto the coming* [or 'hastening the coming'] *of the day of God,"* being well aware that the Lord has not forgotten His promise to return (note 2 Pet. 3:3–4), but knowing also that He is *"longsuffering . . . not willing that any should perish, but that all should come to repentance,"* and accounting that *"the longsuffering of our Lord is salvation"* (2 Pet. 3:12, 9, 15).

One of these days — probably soon — it will finally be true that — *"the fulness of the Gentiles"* will have *"come in"* (Rom. 11:25). This may well correspond closely to when *"the times of the Gentiles"* shall have been *"fulfilled"* and then *"all Israel shall be saved: as it is written, There shall come out of Sion the Deliverer, and shall turn away ungodliness from Jacob: For this is my covenant unto them, when I shall take away their sins. . . . For the gifts and calling of God are without repentance"* (Rom. 11:26–29).

This is still in the future, of course, but perhaps the very near future! The Bible does have a great deal to say about the future of Israel and, indeed, of all the nations, and certainly about those who are citizens of the spiritual nation called *"the church of God."*

It is undoubtedly more difficult to understand what the Scriptures have to say about the future than what they say about the past. Consequently, there are many different schools of interpretation of the prophetic Scriptures, even among those who believe firmly in the full inerrancy and authority of the Bible.

Nevertheless, we need also to try to understand what we can about the future of the nations, because so much of the Bible does deal with the future. We do, indeed, have *"a more sure word of prophecy; whereunto ye do well that ye take heed, as unto a light that shineth in a dark place, until the day dawn, and the day star arise in your hearts"* (2 Pet. 1:19).

In the meantime, we Gentiles can rejoice that Christ, their Messiah, will indeed come some day *"to restore the preserved of Israel,"* and that God the Father has also said to His beloved Son (the same person as the Messiah of Israel) that *"I will also give thee for a light to the Gentiles, that thou mayest be my salvation unto the end of the earth"* (Isa. 49:6).

CHAPTER XII

THE DAY OF GOD'S WRATH

Whether all of the present nations have a future in God's plan, or only some of them, has not been revealed. God, presumably, is still evaluating them in terms of His revealed criteria: (1) their contributions in terms of the dominion mandate; (2) their efforts in seeking God; (3) their treatment of the Jews; and (4) their response to the missions mandate (implied, rather than explicit, based on the initial command to Christ's disciples when He first sent them forth to evangelize: *"Whosoever shall not receive you, nor hear your words, when ye depart out of that house or city, shake off the dust of your feet"* (Matt. 10:14). Their future, of course, in reference to their *"time appointed"* is in the hands of God, as far as individual nations are concerned.

The Bible does have much to say, however, about the future of nations in general. But this raises the question as to how to interpret these prophetic Scriptures. There are many different interpretations, and it is well for any expositor to hold his own interpretation somewhat lightly. The intent in the discussion here in this book is to take them literally, as far as possible. The historical records in the Bible are actual records of real events that really happened in the past, just as described. Also, the many prophecies relating to Christ's first coming were all literally fulfilled (His virgin birth, His birth in Bethlehem, His crucifixion and substitutionary death, His resurrection on the third day, etc.). Therefore, unless otherwise indicated in the Bible itself, future events should be taken literally also. At least, that is the intended interpretation herein.

It would seem that this literal approach would indicate, first of all, that Christ could return at any time, so that we should always be ready. *"Abide in him; that, when he shall appear, we may have confidence, and not be ashamed before him at his coming"* (1 John 2:28). *"Watch therefore"* (Matt. 24:42), He said, quite often.

When the Lord does return, many events are predicted to take place over a period of time, just as was the case with His first coming. The first such event, as just pointed out, being unpredictable as to its time, may possibly be what has come to be called the "Rapture" of all believers, both dead and living. *"The dead in Christ shall rise first: Then we which are alive and remain shall be caught up together with them in the clouds, to meet the Lord in the air"* (1 Thess. 4:16–17).

This event has been called a "sign-less event," since it may occur without advance notice or warning signs. On the other hand, the Bible does give *many* signs of the end times, and many of them are being fulfilled today. The climactic event of Christ's second coming will, in fact, be immediately preceded by great signs in the heavens, so *that* event is definitely *not* a sign-less event. *"Then shall appear the sign of the Son of man in heaven . . . and they shall see the Son of man coming in the clouds of heaven with power and great glory"* (Matt. 24:30).

Many of the other signs may occur either before or after the Rapture, or both, but our interest here is particularly in the prophecies dealing with the nations. Many prophecies, for example, particularly in the Old Testament, say that many Israelites will return home in the last days from that nation's long worldwide dispersal among the other nations, but it was not stated whether that would happen before or after the Rapture. The same uncertainty applies to certain other prophecies about the nations.

Gog and Magog

Consider, for example, the famous Gog/Magog prophecy of Ezekiel 38–39. The prophet sees a time *"in the latter years"* (Ezek. 38:8) after Israel is back as a nation in its promised land, when it is suddenly attacked by a powerful confederacy of nations led by Gog of the land of Magog. The nations involved are listed by name in terms of their identities in the time of Ezekiel, but their modern geographical equivalents would seem to be Russia (the leader), Iran, Ethiopia, Libya, and (probably) the Muslim nations of the former Soviet Union. It will look as if Israel is doomed as it faces this powerful coalition.

There is another chapter of Scripture (Ps. 83) which speaks of a similar confederacy going against Israel, with the purpose to *"cut them off from being a nation; that the name of Israel may be no more in remembrance"* (Ps. 83:4). That this attack is also in the end times is indicated by the fact that the end result of this invasion is *"that men may know that thou, whose name alone is JEHOVAH, art the most High over all the earth"* (Ps. 83:18). The invasion of Gog and the nations with him ends similarly: *"Thus saith the Lord GOD . . . I will be known in the eyes of many nations, and they shall know that I am the LORD"* (Ezek. 38:17–23).

In both cases, the invasion against Israel is said to be defeated by divine intervention. *"As the fire burneth a wood, and as the flame setteth the mountains on fire; So persecute them with thy tempest, and make them afraid with thy storm"* (Ps. 83:14–15). *"Surely in that day there shall be a great shaking in the land of Israel . . . and the mountains shall be thrown down . . . and I will rain upon him, and upon his bands, and upon the many people that are with him, an overflowing rain, and great hailstones, fire, and brimstone"* (Ezek. 38:19–22).

Thus, there are, seemingly, two confederacies invading Israel in the last days, both ending in God's supernatural destruction of Israel's enemies and the resulting widespread acknowledgement that God is the Most High over the earth.

The two confederacies are apparently composed of two different sets of nations. Again, translating the ancient names into their modern geographical equivalents, the invading host in Psalm 83 seems to consist of the nations immediately surrounding Israel — Jordan, Saudi Arabia, the Palestinian Authority, Lebanon, Iraq, etc.

In view of the similar outcomes of these two invasions, both being of unending global impact, it seems probable that they are really two phases of the same operation. Perhaps the smaller nations immediately surrounding Israel (all of which, currently, are Muslim nations, each largely dominated by Muslim literalists) are the first to attack. Then the larger nations, farther away geographically but also largely Muslim (even Russia, to some extent) and sharing a common hatred and envy regarding Israel, decide to join in the invasion, one purpose at least being *"to take a spoil"* (Ezek. 38:12).

What about the nations of Europe and America? Apparently a few have words of remonstration to lodge against the action (Ezek. 38:13), but their modern identity is uncertain (*"the merchants of Tarshish, with all the young lions thereof"*) *may* mean Europe and America, but it is not certain. The original Tarshish was a grandson of Japheth who apparently had established his own family somewhere in Europe, probably either Spain or England, and both of these countries eventually became noted for their maritime trade and their important colonies in America. Sheba and Dedan were in the Arabian peninsula, so it may be that certain important Muslim nations (e.g., Saudi Arabia, Egypt) do not support the invasion.

In any case, the prophesied reaction in support of Israel is minimal, with no suggestion of military help. At this present writing (December 2002), it does seem that the United States is Israel's only friend in her confrontation with the Muslim world, and surely one would expect the United States, the world's most powerful nation, immediately to fly to Israel's defense in such a situation.

Not necessarily. In recent years, America's friendship and support of Israel has been encouraged mostly by Bible-believing Christians, who believe that God's hand had been invisibly responsible for Israel's reestablishment as a nation in her ancient homeland. More and more of America's commercial leaders (sensitive to the need for Muslim oil) and academic elite (highly unimpressed by biblical considerations and very much committed to the United Nations and its goal of world government) are shifting away from providing further aid to Israel.

Now suppose that Bible-believing Christians are all suddenly removed from the world, via the Rapture. It is very likely that, along with the confusion this could generate everywhere, America's support of Israel would quickly deteriorate to little more than expressions of concern. The only hope for Israel's deliverance would be divine intervention. If, on the other hand, this prophesied invasion should take place *before* the Rapture, it does seem almost certain that the United States would quickly provide military assistance to Israel, even if it meant World War III. This scenario seems to support the belief that the Gog/Magog affair will take place very soon after the Rapture. Another point of interest is that so many weapons will have been used by the invading armies that *"they shall burn them with fire seven years"* (Ezek. 39:9) after God has defeated the invaders. It is possible that this is the same period described elsewhere as Daniel's 70th week (Dan. 9:27), which we shall examine shortly.

In any case, when God miraculously saves Israel, this particular event will likely result in the essential elimination of the Muslim nations, and probably the Islamic religion, as well as Russia and her satellites, as significant forces in world affairs.

The European Nations in the Last Days

But the (falsely) so-called Christian nations of the West will not have been eliminated. Once Russia and the more important Muslim nations have been essentially reduced to unimportance, the other European nations will, by process of elimination if nothing else, be greatly expanded in influence and relative power. The United States and other American nations will probably be forced to accept European domination if they still exist (there is at least the possibility of their prior elimination as a power by nuclear, biologic, or chemical attack; perhaps that is the reason why such an important nation as the United States seems not to be mentioned at all in the Bible).

The prophecies in Daniel and Revelation seem to relate specifically to these western nations in the end times. Daniel and Ezekiel were the two prophets during Judah's exile in Babylon, and we have already looked briefly at the main end-time prophecy of Ezekiel (chapters 38 and 39). Several chapters in Daniel (chapters 2, 7–12) relate at least partially to the nations in those coming climactic years of the last days, so we must now look briefly at these.

The basic outline was given to Babylon's King Nebuchadnezzar and then interpreted to him through Daniel. As already mentioned, there were to be four dominating world empires in the future: Babylon, Medo-Persia, Greece, and Rome, in that order, with Rome being the most powerful and extensive, and continuing in her power and influence until God himself would set up His own kingdom over all the earth.

These four earthly kingdoms would each dominate only the biblical "world" of main concern to the Bible writers, but the kingdom to be established ultimately by God would fill the whole earth. The fourth kingdom, Rome, was still in power when *"God sent his only begotten Son into the world"* (1 John 4:9), only to have Him scorned and crucified by those He came to save, both Jews and Gentiles.

Rome's influence, according to Daniel's interpretation, will continue in her dominating influence until Christ returns and God does set up His eternal global kingdom. That influence would change in character, however, from one of politico-military control to one of legal and cultural nature. Historically, the political Roman Empire split into two divisions, one dominated by Greek influence headed at Constantinople, the other at Rome and dominated by Latin influence. Then came the Renaissance, with its goal of reestablishing Greco-Roman culture throughout Europe and the West.

Even as world power seemed to gravitate to England, Spain, and their American "daughter" nations, the languages, legal systems, military systems, religions, and societal cultures in general were essentially extensions of old Rome. Thus, in an important sense, Rome still dominates the world, and will continue to do so until Christ returns to establish His own kingdom. The Roman and Greek Catholic churches have, of course, played significant roles in this extension.

However, Nebuchadnezzar's dream image included a very significant change right at the end, as the two iron legs (denoting the eastern and western divisions of the once-unified Roman Empire, suddenly change into two feet and ten toes. In these, the iron of the legs is mixed with potter's clay, indicating the last form of the Roman kingdom would be still in two divisions, but would be *"partly strong, and partly broken,"* with the centralized power of the state mingled with *"the seed of men"* (Dan. 2:42–43), perhaps an allusion to the mixing of monarchical and democratic governance, or religious and humanistic cultures.

Thus, it seems that, just before the return of Christ to set up His own kingdom, the world will be dominated by ten kingdoms, five in the east (perhaps Greece, Russia, Germany, China, and Japan) and five in the west (perhaps England, America, France, Spain, and Italy). This is all still in the future, of course, so this suggested lineup may well turn out to be something quite different in actuality. The role that may be played in any such development by the United Nations Organization, the currently developing European Union, the North Atlantic Treaty Organization, the World Bank, and other such internationalist movements and organizations is highly uncertain at this time, but could well turn out to be significant.

There are, of course, more than ten significant nations in the world today. Furthermore, some of the nations suggested above (e.g., Russia, America, China, Japan) were never really a part of the old Roman Empire, though the influence of Rome has been significant in almost every nation to some degree, so it is impossible to be dogmatic. Past history is hard enough to understand, but interpreting the prophecies of future history is even more uncertain.

It does seem, at least, that biblical prophecy, not only in Nebuchadnezzar's dream, but also in Daniel 7 and Revelation 7, 13, and 17, points to an end-time world in which ten nations will somehow be of special importance. However, these nations and others will then decide to unite under the leadership of one very talented and charismatic individual, who will in effect become king of the world. In the Bible, he is called *"the prince that shall come"* (Dan. 9:26), but also *"a king of fierce countenance"* (Dan. 8:23), *"that man of sin . . . the son of perdition"* (2 Thess. 2:3, *"antichrist"* (1 John 2:18), *"the abomination of desolation"* (Matt. 24:15), and various other names, but especially *"the beast that ascendeth out of the bottomless pit"* (Rev. 11:7).

In the prophecy of Daniel 7, written during the reign of Belshazzar, these ten kings of the end time are symbolized as ten horns on the head of a dreadful beast. The same is true in Revelation 13:1, except that the ten horns are now seen as growing out of seven heads on the beast. The *"seven heads and ten horns"* are said also to be on *"a great red dragon"* in Revelation 12:3, and then the dragon is *"called the Devil, and Satan, which deceiveth the whole world"* (Rev. 12:9). In Revelation 17:12, the ten horns are again said to be ten kings, who will *"give their power and strength unto the beast"* in order to *"make war with the Lamb"* (Rev. 17:13–14).

Although full understanding of these and other related prophecies must await their fulfillment, it does seem clear enough that these ten prominent nations of the last days will be joined also by many other *"peoples, and multitudes, and nations, and tongues"* (Rev. 17:15) in trying to dethrone the Lamb, which is the same as trying to dethrone God. This goal has been Satan's goal from the beginning, and his long war against God will finally come to a climax on a great plain called Megiddo near a mountain called Har-Megiddo (the "Mount of Megiddo," or Armageddon), some sixty miles north of Jerusalem.

Satan will at that time send demonic messengers *"which go forth unto the kings of the earth and of the whole world, to gather them to the battle of that great day of God Almighty. . . . And he gathered them together into a place called in the Hebrew tongue Armageddon"* (Rev. 16:14–16).

And there at Armageddon finally will be the doom of all the Gentile nations of the world, in their present form at least. The apostle John, in his great prophetic vision, summarized it thus.

> *And I saw the beast, and the kings of the earth, and their armies, gathered together to make war against him that sat on the horse, and against his army. And the beast was taken, and with him the false prophet that wrought miracles before him . . . These both were cast alive into a lake of fire burning with brimstone. And the remnant were slain with the sword of him that sat upon the horse, which sword proceeded out of his mouth: and all the fowls were filled with their flesh* (Rev. 19:19–21).

This great event, which will also include *"the kings of the east"* (Rev. 16:12), will occur right at the end of a climactic period in world history, called by Christ a period of *"great tribulation, such as was not since the beginning of the world to this time, no, nor ever shall be"* (Matt. 24:21).

The 70th Week of Daniel

It is not possible in a small book such as this to deal with all the Scriptures (in both the Old and New Testaments) that apply to this coming Great Tribulation period, for there are a great many of them, and there are already scores of books available on the various interpretations of the end-time prophecies. Our focus here is on God's dealings with the world's nations *as nations*. That period (or at least its beginning) is frequently called *"the day of the Lord"* (e.g., Joel 1:15; 1 Thess. 5:2). It is also called *"the great day of his wrath"* (Rev. 6:17) and various other things, all descriptive of the fact that, after many centuries of patience with the Gentile nations, God is finally going to judge and punish them for rebelling and opposing Him and His people all through the ages.

It is important to realize that this period — the Great Tribulation — is a time of God's wrath on the unbelieving world, not a time for chastening believers or purifying the church. *"For God hath not appointed us to wrath, but to obtain salvation by our Lord Jesus Christ"* (1 Thess. 5:9). *"Because thou hast kept the word of my patience, I also will keep thee from the hour of temptation, which shall come upon all the world, to try them that dwell upon the earth"* (Rev. 3:10). These and other passages would seem to indicate that all genuine Christians will be taken out of the world before God's wrath is unleashed on it, just as those many generations who had already been taken out of the world through death, all having suffered tribulations of one form or another.

Many will accept Christ during this awful period of judgment on the earth, and they will indeed suffer along with the others, not only having to endure the various physical convulsions God will be sending on the earth but also becoming special objects of the wrath of the beast as he and his satanic master are desperately trying to defeat God.

But what about the nation of Israel during that period? Even assuming the Moslem nations are no longer a danger, the phenomenon of anti-Semitism will soon have become worldwide again, as that old serpent seeks to destroy God's chosen people and thereby defeat God's promises. *"Alas! for that day is great, so that none is like it: it is even the time of Jacob's trouble; but he shall be saved out of it"* (Jer. 30:7). *"And at that time . . . there shall be a time of trouble, such as never was since there was a nation even to that same time: and at that time thy people shall be delivered, every one that shall be found written in the book"* (Dan. 12:1).

It will not seem that way at first, however. When the Moslem coalition led by Gog is defeated supernaturally, as discussed earlier in this chapter, there will be a short time of favorable world reaction toward Israel and the God who miraculously delivered their nation from destruction.

This will also be the time when the western nations, evidently led by the "big ten," will be organizing and turning over their nations to the leadership of the great charismatic prince who will be able, they think, finally to engineer world peace and security under the banner, probably, of the United Nations Organization, or some similar successor organization. But *"when they shall say, Peace and safety; then sudden destruction cometh upon them, as travail upon a woman with child; and they shall not escape"* (1 Thess. 5:3). And this period of trouble, tribulation, and destruction is apparently going to last for seven long years.

That number is derived mainly from Daniel's famous prophecy of the 70 weeks yet remaining of God's special dealings with His elect nation Israel. The angel Gabriel was sent to Daniel to convey this marvelous prophecy, while Daniel (now a very old man) was still among the exiles in Babylon, which by that time was under Medo-Persian rule.

> *. . . from the going forth of the commandment to restore and to build Jerusalem* [given by Artaxerxes in about 446 B.C.] *unto the Messiah the Prince shall be seven weeks* [that is, seven "sevens" of years, a period in which the city and its walls were rebuilt and the last Old Testament book, Malachi, was written], *and threescore and two weeks* [a period of 434 more years, ending in about A.D. 30, allowing that the "years" were probably prophetic years of 360 days each] . . . *And after* [the] *threescore and two weeks shall Messiah be cut off, but not for himself* (Dan. 9:25–26).

This is a prophecy that has been wonderfully fulfilled, Messiah having come to Jerusalem on the date predicted over 500 years before it happened, but having then been *"cut off,"* not accepted by Israel as her promised king but crucified instead. Then, the prophecy continued as follows:

> *. . . and the people of the prince that shall come shall destroy the city and the sanctuary* [fulfilled by their Roman rulers a few years after Messiah's crucifixion]: *and the end thereof shall be with a flood* [this word is usually translated "overflowing" and is often used metaphorically; thus it probably refers here to the global dispersion of the Israelites from Jerusalem], *and unto the end of the war desolations are determined* (Dan. 9:26).

This prophetic time specified of 69 weeks of years thus far has been literally fulfilled. But then several things are said to happen before the 70th week begins. Gabriel had said that, *"Seventy weeks are determined upon thy people* [that is, the nation of Israel] *and upon thy holy city, to finish the transgression, and to make an end of sins, and to make reconciliation for iniquity, and to bring in everlasting righteousness, and to seal up the vision and prophecy, and to anoint the most Holy"* (Dan. 9:24).

But then, after Messiah was to be *"cut off"* and the Romans were to destroy Jerusalem and its temple, and then wars and desolations to continue for an unspecified length of time — only then would *"the prince that shall come"* have the power and make the decision to *"confirm the covenant with many for one week"* (Dan. 9:26–27).

Thus, there is clearly an unknown period of time between the 69th and 70th weeks of Daniel's prophecy. That period has already lasted almost 2,000 years, but it does seem that it could end soon, and the 70th week begin.

For that 70th week almost certainly includes the time of Jacob's trouble mentioned by Jeremiah and the Great Tribulation mentioned by Christ. It will begin innocuously enough with the coming prince, who will have come into world power with all nations submitting to his leadership, making a seven-year treaty with the Israelites (who are, after Gog's amazing defeat, looked upon with respect such as they had not known since the days of King Solomon) to rebuild their temple and restore the ancient sacrificial system instituted by Moses. However, the prince suddenly will decide to abrogate his treaty with Israel after only three and a half years.

> . . . *in the midst of the week he shall cause the sacrifice and the oblation to cease, and for the overspreading of abominations he shall make it desolate, even until the consummation, and that determined shall be poured upon the desolate* (Dan. 9:27).

By this time, after 3½ years of the treaty, with the temple and its ancient worship reestablished, the great prince will decide that no god should be worshiped except Satan, and himself as Satan's human representative. He will consolidate his treaty with the various Gentile nations and abrogate his treaty with Israel. *"And then shall that Wicked [One] be revealed"* (2 Thess. 2:8). He will be clearly revealed to all with eyes to see and who somehow have a little familiarity with Bible prophecy, as *"that man of sin . . . the son of perdition: Who opposeth and exalteth himself above all that is called God, or that is worshipped; so that he as God sitteth in the temple of God, shewing himself that he is God"* (2 Thess. 2:3–4).

Here is the ultimate blasphemy and idolatry — the abomination of desolation! And yet the ungodly masses in the nations *"worshipped the dragon which gave power unto the beast: and they worshipped the beast"* (Rev. 13:4). *"And power was given unto him to continue forty and two months . . . and power was given him over all kindreds, and tongues, and nations"* (Rev. 13:5–7).

The whole world will finally fulfill Satan's great ambition — to be recognized as God, incredible as it may seem. Actually, they will have no choice; a second beast, called the false prophet, will *"cause that as many as would not worship the image of the beast should be killed"* (Rev. 13:15). So it will be a choice between becoming a satanist, or fleeing to the desert, or being executed.

The Lord Jesus Christ, foreseeing all these ominous events, said: *"When ye therefore shall see the abomination of desolation, spoken of by Daniel the prophet, stand in the holy place . . . Then let them which be in Judæa flee into the mountains . . . For then shall be great tribulation, such as was not since the beginning of the world to this time, no, nor ever shall be"* (Matt. 24:15–21).

At this point, Daniel's 70th week will have 3½ years still to go, and these will be dreadful years. The world will be undergoing a succession of terrible calamities sent by God, at the same time that the beast is seeking to exterminate both the Jews and any Gentiles who dare accept Christ. All of this is described in the graphic words used by John in recounting his visions, as described in his Book of Revelation.

We have already noted the tragic end of the Gentile nations at Armageddon. With Israel, however, these years will be purifying years, as they are being brought back to God. Apparently, under the teaching first of God's two ancient witnesses (probably Enoch and Elijah, preserved in heaven without dying until sent back to earth to complete their ministries) and then under the teaching of 144,000 Israelites specially prepared somehow to accept Christ themselves and then preach to those of their kinsmen, the Israelites, who have managed to escape the Beast, will finally be ready to acknowledge Christ when He returns.

See Revelation 7 and 11 — then 14 — for the fascinating accounts from which these deductions can be drawn.

Then, when the Lord Jesus — their rejected Messiah and Savior — finally appears *"immediately after the tribulation of those days . . . in the clouds of heaven with power and great glory,"* (Matt. 24:29–30), the nation in effect will be born again, and *"all Israel shall be saved"* (Rom. 11:26).

> *And I will pour upon the house of David and upon the inhabitants of Jerusalem, the spirit of grace and of supplications: and they shall look upon me whom they have pierced, and they shall mourn for him, as one mourneth for his only son, and shall be in bitterness for him, as one that is in bitterness for his firstborn. . . . In that day there shall be a fountain opened to the house of David and to the inhabitants of Jerusalem for sin and for uncleanness . . . They shall call on my name, and I will hear them: I will say, It is my people: and they shall say, The LORD is my God* (Zech. 12:10–13:9).

CHAPTER XIII

NATIONS IN THE AGES TO COME

At Armageddon, the armies of all the Gentile nations will be destroyed, and the Lord Jesus will terminate the many earthly events of His second coming with that great battle. He will finally be recognized by Israel as her long-awaited Messiah and Savior, ready to assume the throne of David, just as the angelic messenger had promised immediately prior to His first coming. At that time, Gabriel announced to His human mother:

> Behold, thou shalt conceive in thy womb, and bring forth a son, and shalt call his name JESUS. He shall be great, and shall be called the Son of the Highest: and the Lord God shall give unto him the throne of his father David: And he shall reign over the house of Jacob for ever; and of his kingdom there shall be no end (Luke 1:31–33).

But now, there must first be a transition from the violence and chaos of His triumphant coming in power and glory to the establishment of His worldwide kingdom on earth. Although the armies will have been destroyed, most of the citizens of the nations will have not been in the armies, and though multitudes will have previously died in the various terrestrial catastrophes and in the purges of the beast, there will still be significant numbers of people left in the two hundred or so nations of the earth. Many will be willing to follow the beast and receive his mark and, even though not in the armies directly, will have supported his government (although some no doubt will have resisted and managed to escape his emissaries). The military leaders will all be dead, but at least most of the political, educational, and business leaders will be alive and will have been supportive of his anti-Christian and anti-Jewish purges. So what will happen to all this remaining population?

Judgment of the Nations

There is a very important future event described for us by Christ himself shortly before His crucifixion. This event has been called "the judgment of the nations," and will apparently take place very soon after His triumphant return to earth.

> *When the Son of man shall come in his glory . . . before him shall be gathered all nations: and he shall separate them one from another, as a shepherd divideth his sheep from the goats* (Matt. 25:31–32).

These "nations" are apparently composed of the men and women still living on the earth after Armageddon. This scene is obviously not the same as the judgment of the resurrected dead by God at the end of the age or of Christians as Christ's judgment seat. Christ — actually probably His angels — will somehow have gathered people from all over the world, separating them into two great companies to receive Christ's judgment. One company — called the "sheep" — will be invited to *"inherit the kingdom prepared for you from the foundation of the world"* (Matt. 25:34). The other — the "goats" — will be told, *"Depart from me, ye cursed, into everlasting fire, prepared for the devil and his angels"* (Matt. 25:41).

The first group is composed of true, born-again, believing Christians, for they will *"go away . . . into life eternal,"* while the second contains only lost and unrepentant sinners who will *"go away into everlasting punishment"* (Matt. 25:46). The evidence of their saving faith — or lack of it — is the way they have been dealing with those whom Christ calls *"the least of these my brethren"* (Matt. 25:40), helping them (or not) with food, shelter, and care while sick or imprisoned during the period of great trouble.

The Greek word translated *"nations"* is the same word translated *"Gentiles,"* depending on context. Thus, the nations called here by Christ are Gentile nations, and do not include Israel. There has long been disagreement among Bible expositors as to whether *ethnos* here means the Gentile nations as such, or rather the individual citizens of those nations.

As a matter of fact, it could well mean both. That is, only certain nations will inherit the earthly kingdom; the others will no longer be allowed to continue as nations in the ensuing age of the earthly kingdom of Christ. Individual men and women in the kingdom will, during the Great Tribulation just ending, have accepted Christ and been given life eternal, and all others (regardless of their earthly citizenship) will be executed (that had already been the fate of all those in the armies at Armageddon) and their souls dispatched to hades to await the final judgment.

As to the identity of those called *"my brethren"* by the Lord Jesus, these almost certainly are the Jews, who will have been the special objects of the genocidal purges of the beast for the previous 3½ long years. Those living in Jerusalem and other cities in Israel will have fled to the mountain and desert wilderness south and east of Jerusalem, as Jesus had told his first disciples when predicting this period (Matt. 24:15–26), but the Jews in other countries needed help from those who had become Christians during the first 3½ years of Daniel's 70th week and had been able somehow to escape the purges of the beast themselves.

On some such basis, the Lord Jesus will not only give eternal life to those individual believers who have (no doubt at great risk to themselves) sought to help (and presumably win to faith in Christ) those Jews in their vicinity suffering under the beast's pogroms but also decide which nations will be allowed to continue as nations in the kingdom age.

This tremendous assize was also foreseen in the Old Testament. The prophet Joel saw, in a prophetic vision, *"Multitudes, multitudes in the valley of decision"* (Joel 3:14). That valley of decision seems to be the *"valley of Jehoshaphat,"* somewhere in the general region between Jerusalem and the Dead Sea.

> *For, behold, in those days, and in that time, when I shall bring*
> *again the captivity of Judah and Jerusalem, I will also gather all*

nations, and will bring them down into the valley of Jehoshaphat, and will plead with them there for my people and for my heritage Israel, whom they have scattered among the nations, and parted my land. . . . Let the heathen be wakened, and come up to the valley of Jehoshaphat: for there will I sit to judge all the heathen round about (Joel 3:1–12).

According to the prophet Isaiah, God had said *"I will gather all nations and tongues; and they shall come, and see my glory"* (Isa. 66:18).

Then *"the wicked shall be turned into hell, and all the nations that forget God"* (Ps. 9:17). Nations can hardly be sent into hell (that is, *Sheol*, the great abyss in the deep interior of the earth where departed souls are awaiting judgment) as nations, but the wicked men and women certainly can, including especially the leaders of those apostate nations. As nations, it is clear that the corresponding penalty would have to be the termination of their existence as nations.

There are other judgments mentioned in the Bible, of course, especially the final judgment of all the unsaved dead at God's great white throne, which will finally banish Satan and all sin forever (Rev. 20:11–15). This judgment of the nations, however, has to do only with the people and nations living on earth at the end of the period of great tribulation.

The Restoration of Israel

At this time, Israel will be restored and all of God's promises to her (beginning with those to Abraham) will finally be fulfilled in every detail. She will, indeed, be the world's chief nation, and her king will be the world's king. All living Israelites will also have become Christians, having accepted Christ as national Messiah and personal Savior. Note just a few of the many relevant Scriptures confirming this great event.

And so all Israel shall be saved: as it is written, There shall come out of Sion the Deliverer, and shall turn away ungodliness from Jacob: For this is my covenant with them, when I shall take away their sins (Rom. 11:26–27).

And many people shall go and say, Come ye, and let us go up to the mountain of the LORD, to the house of the God of Jacob;

and he will teach us of his ways, and we will walk in his paths: for out of Zion shall go forth the law, and the word of the LORD from Jerusalem (Isa. 2:3).

And it shall come to pass, that every man that is left of all the nations which came against Jerusalem shall even go up from year to year to worship the King, the LORD of hosts (Zech. 14:16).

And it shall come to pass, if thou shalt hearken diligently unto the voice of the LORD thy God, to observe and to do all his commandments which I command thee this day, that the LORD thy God will set thee on high above all nations of the earth (Deut. 28:1).

Israel shall indeed, in that day, become the holy and righteous nation that God had planned in the beginning. After her thousands of years of rebellion, followed by global dispersion and persecution, climaxed by the terrors of the beast for 3½ years of the Great Tribulation, she will truly have been wholly converted to Christ and the full will of God.

But this shall be the covenant that I will make with the house of Israel; After those days, saith the LORD, I will put my law in their inward parts, and write it in their hearts; and will be their God, and they shall be my people. . . . for I will forgive their iniquity, and I will remember their sin no more (Jer. 31:33–34).

Therefore say unto the house of Israel, Thus saith the LORD GOD . . . A new heart also will I give you . . . And I will put my Spirit within you: and cause you to walk in my statutes, and ye shall keep my judgments, and do them (Ezek. 36:22–27).

All 12 tribes will be together again in the land promised to Abraham long ago. During the reign of the beast, God will have prepared and called twelve thousand witnesses out of each of the 12 tribes (see Rev. 7:4–8), and these will have probably been the chief (human) means used by the Lord to prepare Israel for the triumphant return of Christ and her national conversion.

Whether the 144,000 witnesses will also serve as officials of various ministries in the new kingdom remains to be seen, but we do know that the Lord Jesus Christ himself will reign over Israel and, in fact, over the whole world. *"I shall give thee . . . the uttermost parts of the earth for thy possession,"* the Father had promised the Son at least three thousand years before (Ps. 2:8).

Furthermore, *"at the coming of our Lord Jesus Christ,"* He will be accompanied by *"all his saints"* (1 Thess. 3:13), meaning all the people who long ago had trusted Him as Savior and then had been given resurrection bodies during His second appearing. In some way these also will share His reign.

> *Blessed and holy is he that hath part in the first resurrection: on such the second death had no power, but they shall be priests of God and of Christ, and shall reign with him a thousand years* (Rev. 20:6).

Presumably their ministry as *"kings and priests unto God and his Father"* (Rev. 1:6) will be exercised particularly to the Gentile nations remaining, except probably for the resurrected Israelites among them, whose ministries will probably be toward earthly Israel.

Among the latter will be the 12 apostles, now resurrected and glorified. To them Jesus had promised: *"in the regeneration, when the Son of man shall sit in the throne of his glory, ye also shall sit upon twelve thrones, judging the twelve tribes of Israel"* (Matt. 19:28).

Furthermore, King David will also have been resurrected (possibly with the Old Testament saints right after the resurrection of Christ — see Matt. 27:52–53), and he will sit on Israel's throne along with His greater Son, the Messiah, as a sort of co-regent over Israel with Christ, who will also be ruling the whole world. *"Afterward shall the children of Israel return, and seek the LORD their God, and David their king; and shall fear the LORD and his goodness in the latter days"* (Hos. 3:5).

The Gentile Nations in the Kingdom Age

The Kingdom Age (according to Rev. 20:2–7) will continue for a thousand years. This may seem like a long time, but our present Church Age has already lasted about twice that long. In addition to the nation of Israel, there will be a certain number of Gentile nations allowed by Christ to participate in this Kingdom Age (or Millennium). The identity of these nations will have been specified by Christ at His "judgment of the nations," as discussed earlier in this chapter.

Presumably His determination as to which nations will continue will be based upon the four criteria suggested by Him as indicative of divine favor (effectiveness in carrying out the dominion and missionary mandates, and treatment of the Jews and the Christians).

Americans would hope and believe that the United States would fare better in such an evaluation than most others and thus would be one of the ongoing nations, despite the widespread apathy and skepticism in America in recent years. But this, of course, will be Christ's decision.

In any case, the "kings" of the nations (whether called by this title or some other) will be responsible to the king at Jerusalem. Again note Zechariah 14:16. *"Every one that is left of all the nations . . . shall even go up from year to year to worship the King, the* LORD *of hosts, and to keep the feast of tabernacles."*

It will still not be a perfect world, as its inhabitants will still be in the natural flesh and thus subject to the same old sins of the flesh, even though Satan (and presumably his angels with him) will be confined in the great abyss for the thousand years of the Kingdom Age (Rev. 20:2). It will, however, be a peaceful world, for the Lord and His saints will *"rule them with a rod of iron"* (Rev. 2:27) and will not permit crime or wickedness to flourish. *"Nation shall not lift up sword against nation, neither shall they learn war any more . . . and none shall make them afraid"* (Mic. 4:3–4). *"They shall not hurt nor destroy in all my holy mountain: for the earth shall be full of the knowledge of the"* LORD, *as the waters cover the sea"* (Isa. 11:9).

There will also be wonderful changes in the earth itself, many of which will be the result of the vast upheavals of the tribulation period.

> *Every valley shall be exalted, and every mountain and hill shall be made low: and the crooked shall be made straight, and the rough places plain* (Isa. 40:4).

> *The wilderness and the solitary place shall be glad for them; and the desert shall rejoice, and blossom as the rose. . . . for in the wilderness shall waters break out, and streams in the desert* (Isa. 35:1–6).

> *And I will . . . cause the evil beasts to cease out of the land: and they shall dwell safely in the wilderness, and sleep in the woods.*

. . . and I will cause the shower to come down in his season; there shall be showers of blessing (Ezek. 34:25–26).

There are many other passages describing the beauties of the millennial world and the perfection of its environment. Furthermore, all the men and women of the nations allowed to enter the millennium will be true believing Christians. Israelites and Gentiles will know and gladly serve the Lord and His Word. One would suppose the world would be perfect from then on.

They will also have the Lord Jesus there in person on the earth again, as well as the redeemed and resurrected saints of all the ages, all *"the just* [that is, justified] *men made perfect"* (Heb. 12:23). Although the permanent homes of the latter will be in the heavenly mansions prepared by Christ for them (John 14:2, 3), they will have been given ministries of instruction and judgment for those still in their mortal bodies, and still subject to sin and death. *"The saints shall judge the world,"* Paul had said (1 Cor. 6:2), and John had said that the Lord Jesus *"hath made us kings and priests"* (Rev. 1:6) and that in his great vision of the future he *"saw thrones, and they sat upon them, and judgment was given unto them"* (Rev. 20:4).

What an amazing future we Christians have! We would do well to prepare now as best we can.

One would think that the mortal citizens of the millennial nations, with an ideal world of peace and prosperity in which to live and work, will be perfectly happy and will serve the Lord with total commitment throughout their long lives (longevity itself would be greatly increased!).

But not necessarily so with the second and later generations of children born during the Millennium. As the memory of the traumatic events of the past begin to fade, and young people have to rely on the tales of the parents and perhaps the teachings of the resurrected saints, the old fallen nature will begin to reassert itself. Rebellious attitudes will simmer and eventually surface. Overt sin will initially be rare and God's grace will allow ready forgiveness for a long time, *"but the sinner being an hundred years old shall be accursed"* (Isa. 65:20).

With the world completely at peace for a thousand years, and with an ideal environment, there will almost certainly be great advances in science, medicine, technology, commerce, and education. The dominion mandate will be carried out more widely and effectively than in all previous ages. In a very significant way, it will be the kingdom of God on earth, with His will being done on earth as it is in heaven!

Well, not quite! There will still be sin and rebellion in the unregenerate human heart. Each person will still need to be spiritually reborn through faith in Christ as his sin-bearing personal Savior, and many in later generations, with everything going so well, will see no need for this. The old blood sacrifices will have been reinstituted in the new temple in Jerusalem, presumably to remind men of the eternal truth that Christ (now their global King) once had to suffer and die to save their souls, and that *"without shedding of blood is no remission"* (Heb. 9:22).

Furthermore, *"every one that is left of all the nations"* will be expected to go to Jerusalem for *"the feast of tabernacles"* each year *"to worship the King,"* with physical calamities to be visited on those nations that do not (Zech. 14:1–19). As the world population begins to grow to the point that Jerusalem could not hold all who might come, perhaps each nation could send delegations to Jerusalem, and each nation could keep the feast of tabernacles in its own homeland, simultaneously in conformity with the observation in Jerusalem.

Nevertheless, the spirit of rebellion will continue to fester in the hearts of the younger generations, even though outward rebellion will be prevented. Finally, Satan (who has been confined in the great abyss of hades throughout the millennium) *"shall be loosed out of his prison, And shall go out to deceive the nations"* once more (Rev. 20:7–8).

And amazingly, despite a thousand years of an almost perfect environment in which all could prosper, Satan will be able to gather a tremendous host of human followers to besiege and attack Jerusalem, still apparently hoping they could defeat and dethrone Christ.

Satan, the great deceiver and liar, will still be deceptively lying to himself most of all, unrepentant in his belief that he can somehow become the god of the universe.

At this point, however, God's patience will have finally come to an end, and *"fire came down from God out of heaven, and devoured them"* (Rev. 20:9). That will be the absolute end of all rebellion, whether human or demonic, and therefore of all sin, which derives ultimately from such rebellion.

There are many, many more passages of Scripture that apply primarily to this great coming age of Christ and His kingdom here on earth after He comes again. One could easily devote an entire book to this one subject, and some have tried to do so.

This is all in the future, of course, and as cautioned earlier, one needs to deal somewhat tentatively with prophecies of the future. Things may not turn out quite the way we have interpreted them to predict. That will not be the fault of the prophet, of course, but of the interpreter. One thing we do know, of course, is that the Lord Jesus Christ *will* return to earth and *"in the ages to come,"* He will be demonstrating *"the exceeding riches of his grace in his kindness toward us"* (Eph. 2:7).

Nations in the New Earth

Most of what we know about the age to come after the millennial age is found in the last two chapters of the Bible. And a glorious future it is!

The best thing of all, of course, is that we shall *"ever be with the Lord"* (1 Thess. 4:17). Furthermore, *"there shall be no more death, neither sorrow, nor crying, neither shall there be any more pain"* (Rev. 21:4). And the reason why there is no more death or pain is that in the holy city where we shall live, *"there shall in no wise enter into it any thing that defileth"* (Rev. 21:27). As the apostle Peter said, *"We, according to his promise, look for new heavens and a new earth, wherein dwelleth righteousness"* (2 Pet. 3:13).

The inhabitants of that *"holy city, new Jerusalem, coming down from God out of heaven"* will only be *"they which are written in the Lamb's book of life"* (Rev. 21:2, 27), for *"whosoever was not found written in the book of life was cast into the lake of fire"* (Rev. 20:15). That fiery lake is somewhere far away from the earth, and is the ultimate prison of the devil and his angels as well (Matt. 25:41). Within the holy city will be the "mansions" promised by the Lord Jesus to His disciples (John 14:2–3), which will be their "headquarters," so to speak, in this age to come.

However, they will not simply be resting forever in their eternal homes, for *"His servants shall serve him"* (Rev. 22:3). We have not yet been informed as to what that service may be, but we can be sure it will be both useful and delightful. It will probably be related in some way to the preparations for it that we have made in our work here on earth.

One of the final words from Christ in the Scriptures is that, when He comes, *"my reward is with me, to give every man according as his work shall be"* (Rev. 22:12). Thus, our "reward" in that day will somehow be commensurate with the "service" we shall render there.

There will be much to do in eternity, and we can only speculate about it now. *"The things which God hath prepared for them that love him"* (1 Cor. 2:9) are beyond understanding now. But we can note that God has created a vast universe, with stars (and probably planets) without number, and He has some purpose for all of it. Perhaps the dominion mandate given to Adam and Eve at the creation with reference to our stewardship over the earth was sort of a "pilot project" here, as it were, which can be expanded to cover the entire cosmos there. One can note in awe that we shall have endless time ahead to explore and develop the boundless universe, all to the glory of our great God of creation and redemption. In Christ *"are hid all the treasures of wisdom and knowledge"* (Col. 2:3), and it may always be *"the glory of God to conceal a thing: but the honour of kings is to search out a matter. The heaven for height, and the earth for depth, and the heart of kings is unsearchable"* (Prov. 25:2–3). And there we shall be kings and priests in His service.

Surprisingly perhaps, there will still be nations in the new earth. Although New Jerusalem will have come down onto the earth and will be of tremendous size (apparently about 1,380 miles square and 1,380 miles high), it will certainly not cover the whole surface of the earth — at least on the reasonable assumption that the new earth is essentially the first earth made new again. Thus, there will be extensive land areas outside the holy city, and these will be occupied by nations.

Here is what it says: *"The nations of them which are saved shall walk in the light of it* [that is, of the holy city, where the Lamb himself provides light, physical as well as spiritual]: *and the kings of the earth . . . shall bring the glory and honour of the nations into it"* (Rev. 21:24–26).

Thus, the nations of the new earth are composed of men and women who are saved (and who presumably also have their own personal mansions in the Holy City, prepared for them by the One who saved them and who then prepared those mansions after He returned to heaven following His first coming. Also each "nation" will have a king.

Although it doesn't say so directly, all this would indicate that the nations on the new earth will be the same nations approved by Christ for the millennial earth. This time, however, all their citizens will be born-again Christians and will always be the only citizens of that nation. No new children will be born, since there is no marriage either in heaven or in the new earth, at least so far as revealed in Scripture (note Luke 20:35).

As far as the "kings" of these nations are concerned, these will no doubt be chosen and appointed by the King of kings. Since there will be no sin, there will be no crime or dispute to judge, but presumably someone may need to decide the individual contribution of each nation to the whole divine economy.

Although nations will still be nations as such, they will all serve their Lord in perfect harmony, with no nationalistic rivalries or arguments. Furthermore, the linguistic divisions imposed long ago at Babel will all be dissolved.

> *For then will I turn to the people a pure language, that they may all call upon the name of the* Lord, *to serve him with one consent* (Zeph. 3:9).

And though they have come from every nation — *"a great multitude, which no man could number, of all nations, and kindreds, and people, and tongues"* (Rev. 7:9) — they will all be united in giving praise to their Savior and Lord, saying, *"Blessing, and glory, and wisdom, and thanksgiving, and honour, and power, and might, be unto our God for ever and ever"* (Rev. 7:12).

We shall be among that number! If we have, in our present nation (which we hope will still be a nation in the millennium and in the new earth) believed on Christ in our hearts and acknowledged Him with our lips and lives, then we shall join that great multitude in glory praising and serving Him.

Therefore, *"unto him be glory in the church* [that is, 'the general assembly and church of the firstborn, which are written in heaven' — Heb. 12:23] *by Christ Jesus throughout all ages, world without end. Amen"* (Eph. 3:21).

INDEX OF SUBJECTS

INDEX OF SCRIPTURES

1 JOHN

JUDE

REVELATION